# Learners First

**Dedications**

*Denise:*

*For Tim and our kids, who just accept my crazy journeys without question: I'm very grateful for our life, and I'm proud to call you mine.*

*For my parents, my sisters, my brother, and the rest of our big, beautiful family: Thank you for providing me with a sense of belonging and a home base.*

*For my village of strong, intelligent, beautiful women (many of whom contributed quotes and vignettes for this book): We are worth it and our voices matter! I appreciate you all more than you know.*

*For Dr. Keri: Thank you for being you, authentic, passionate, and kind. I love you!*

*Keri:*

*For David, my best friend and the other half of my Libra scale, who gives me balance; thank you for loving me every day. I love you beyond!*

*For my parents, especially Mommy (I am your little engine that could and did), and my brother, my bonus daughter Laila, all the powerful women in my life (aunties, girlfriends, bonus mothers, sisters-in-law, nieces) who inspire me, and the rest of my family (uncles, cousins, and brothers-in-law), too numerous to mention: Thank you for being the best family. I love all of you!*

*I am surrounded by phenomenally fierce females! This is our journey. Thank you for being supportive.*

*For Dr. Denise: One of my "She-Roes." I love you! On to the next one!!*

*Dedicated to the memory of all my ancestors: I am your dreams fulfilled.*

# Learners First

## Purpose and Practicality in Your Early Years of Teaching

Denise Furlong
Keri Orange-Jones

CORWIN

FOR INFORMATION:

Corwin
A SAGE Company
2455 Teller Road
Thousand Oaks, California 91320
(800) 233-9936
www.corwin.com

SAGE Publications Ltd.
1 Oliver's Yard
55 City Road
London EC1Y 1SP
United Kingdom

SAGE Publications India Pvt. Ltd.
Unit No 323-333, Third Floor, F-Block
International Trade Tower Nehru Place
New Delhi 110 019
India

SAGE Publications Asia-Pacific Pte. Ltd.
18 Cross Street #10-10/11/12
China Square Central
Singapore 048423

Vice President and Editorial Director: Monica Eckman
Acquisitions Editor: Megan Bedell
Senior Content Development Editor: Mia Rodriguez
Content Development and Operations Manager: Lucas Schleicher
Senior Editorial Assistant: Natalie Delpino
Production Editor: Tori Mirsadjadi
Copy Editor: Karin Rathert
Typesetter: C&M Digitals (P) Ltd.
Cover Designer: Scott Van Atta
Marketing Manager: Melissa Duclos



Printed and bound by CPI Group (UK) Ltd, Croydon, CR0 4YY

*Library of Congress Cataloging-in-Publication Data*

Names: Furlong, Denise author | Orange-Jones, Keri author

Title: Learners first : purpose and practicality in your early years of teaching / Denise Furlong, Keri Orange-Jones.

Description: Thousand Oaks, California : Corwin, [2025] | Includes bibliographical references and index.

Identifiers: LCCN 2024057417 | ISBN 9781071964286 paperback | ISBN 9781071964293 epub | ISBN 9781071964309 epub | ISBN 9781071964316 pdf

Subjects: LCSH: Teacher effectiveness | First year teachers | Mentoring in education | Teaching—Philosophy

Classification: LCC LB1025.3 .F855 2025 | DDC 371.102—dc23/eng/20250327

LC record available at https://lccn.loc.gov/2024057417

This book is printed on acid-free paper.

24 25 26 27 28 10 9 8 7 6 5 4 3 2 1

# CONTENTS

# PUBLISHER'S ACKNOWLEDGMENTS

Corwin gratefully acknowledges the contributions of the following reviewers:

Karen Kozy-Landress
Speech/Language Pathologist
Brevard Public Schools
Viera, FL

Deanna McClung
Teacher, NBCT
Elkhorn Area High School
Elkhorn, WI

Melissa Miller
Middle School Science Educator
Randall G. Lynch Middle School
Farmington, AR

Renee Nealon
Elementary School teacher
Petaluma City Schools
Petaluma, CA

# ABOUT THE AUTHORS

**Dr. Denise Furlong** is an assistant professor/director of Advanced Programs for Reading Specialists and ESL for Georgian Court University. She has taught for over twenty-five years in the New Jersey public school system, ranging from kindergarten through 12th grade. She also has mentored and coached both novice and veteran teachers over the years. She is the author of *Voices of Newcomers: Experiences of Multilingual Learners* (Furlong, 2022b). She is a proud member of Delta Kappa Gamma and was the recipient of their Educators Book Award in 2023. She lives at the Jersey Shore with her husband, Tim, her three kids (Ryan, Joey, and Sarah), and their two dogs. You can connect with her on Instagram/Threads @denisefurlong.

**Dr. Keri Orange-Jones** is a middle school assistant principal and adjunct professor at Montclair University and William Paterson University. She has been an educator for twenty-seven years. Keri is also part of the Drew Writing Project and National Writing Project, and a member of Sigma Gamma Rho Sorority. She has offered her insight as a guest speaker on podcasts and several virtual professional learning communities. She has also published blogs and journal articles and contributed to other publications. She is an advocate for equity and accessibility for all students, regardless of socioeconomic status. Additional research interests include teacher education and evaluation, student assessment, positive school culture and climate, and the importance of representation and diversity in the educational field. She lives in New Jersey with her husband David and her bonus daughter Laila. She takes great pride in being a daughter, sister, niece, aunt, cousin and friend. She is also a foodie, loves to travel, and enjoys beach vacations. You can connect with her on Instagram/Threads @drkcorange.

# INTRODUCTION

Education today is an ever-changing journey, and it is critical to continue learning throughout our careers. The resources of the past simply do not address the issues of today and tomorrow. It is important to reframe and reimagine the role of educators to match the diverse needs of learners and their families—as well as the different landscapes of the future. Not only do educators need to have the academic and pedagogical knowledge that is crucial to engage learners in critical thinking and learning, but they must have a comprehensive understanding of the cultural and social contexts of education.

While this book is primarily designed to support educators early in the profession, the reflections and conversations on these topics must be had by educators and stakeholders in all positions and with different levels of experience. This book is designed to encourage activating connections and prior knowledge before learning new concepts (or exploring familiar concepts through a different lens). Each chapter begins with some reflection questions and key vocabulary to understand before reading. Quotes and vignettes from current educators provide context and background perspective to the educational concepts covered. While each chapter addresses a different topic for educators, the common threads of equity, access, respect, and empowerment are laced within every word.

Educators who see themselves as learners engage their students to value questioning, collaboration, and listening over one's lifetime. We designed this book to meet the needs of today's educators with the unique challenges that form the conversations we all must be having. We are two career educators who have served learners, their families, and their teachers through a variety of roles (in a combined total of over 50 years in education!). Throughout our respective educational journeys, we have witnessed shifts in policy, perspectives, strategies, and roles of educators—just to name a few. These experiences inform this guide to what educators need to best meet the needs of the learners and families they serve today.

Denise: Over my career as a public-school teacher, I taught grades K–12 in different educational roles for over twenty-five years. Like Keri, my path in education has taken some unexpected turns, and I am grateful for them. Although I spent much of my career in one district, I did wind up teaching in four different towns over those years—giving me valuable perspectives on the diverse needs of learners in different areas. My work in mentoring new teachers and eventually as an instructional coach led me to taking the leap to working at a university full time as an assistant professor of education. At the university level, I supervise student teachers, and I teach graduate students seeking additional certifications in literacy and language education. It was then that I saw a need for authentic resources to support educators entering our profession. Previous to this project with Keri, I wrote a book for teachers of multilingual learners called *Voices of Newcomers: Experiences of Multilingual Learners.* It was through all these experiences that I realized the value of mentorship and support for *all* educators (novice and veteran!) in ways to keep learning and growing.

Keri: Being in the education profession happened quite by chance. I worked in corporate finance after college graduation and fell into this honorable vocation. As an alternate route teacher, I always looked at education through a different lens, one of innovation and experimentation. Now, after twenty-seven years, I am still excited about teaching our youth. But I am also passionate about guiding educators, especially novice educators, because they need our support. Teacher retention is an area of concern, and my hope is to assist those who desire to stay in the profession. I have mentored novice educators, and I teach in teacher education departments at two universities. In addition, I also guide educators who wish to transition to supervisory and administrative roles. Every chapter in our book will be useful to anyone in this profession. Much of the information included in this book is things that I wish I knew or experienced in my early years. This book is not a passion project. It is our attempt at *paying it forward* and providing support to those who desire it!

As you read this book—whether it is for a course, a mentorship program, or as personal preparation as you enter our profession—please consider the following statements as you dive into each of the concepts and vignettes.

- Our own education (and life!) experiences are valid, and our voice is valuable. Those of the learners and families we serve may be different from our perceptions, but they are no less important. Setting up our own opinions and background as a starting point is a great place to begin as we grow and understand different perspectives. In other words, identifying our own thoughts and experiences before diving into learning about others is crucial in learning about ourselves and others.

- No one knows everything, and being open to learning and listening is crucial at all points in our lives. We don't always have to know all the answers. Admitting we don't know or that we may be wrong is sometimes difficult but can be a key part of our own growth. If educators get to the point that they feel they are the experts and cannot learn from the learners and families they serve—or from their colleagues—there may be little value in teaching for them. The term *lifelong learner* may be a bit overused or cliche, but it is authentically what keeps educators fresh and constantly improving their craft. As you reflect on the chapter addressing professional learning, you will see that this is essential throughout your career.
- Uncomfortable conversations are key to growth. When there are questions or statements that make you feel uneasy or queasy in your stomach, it is time to learn more about this topic. While we are learning, we don't have to always speak, and we don't have to share our thoughts right away—but finding colleagues with whom you can have these safe conversations in which you are all learning and growing may be helpful. If you are asked for your point of view as you are still researching information, it is perfectly acceptable to respond that you are still *listening and learning* as you gather your thoughts. This may be particularly connected to the chapters on being an equity innovator, the *alphabet* acronyms, and learners with diverse needs.
- There are many things that new educators must navigate in their first years, such as evaluations, observations, assessments, and maintaining their own positive social emotional mental health. Keeping this book handy as you confront these benchmarks in your first years may remind you of ways to best maneuver them. While these formalities vary in different states and districts, we share some key tips and tricks to support you in these areas. Remember that these are learning experiences and you may struggle at times—and that is OK. Kindness to yourself as you are learning and listening to the signals of your body are key to your health and progress.
- Instead of a delineated focus on classroom management as many resources have done in the past, we maintain that every topic covered in this book will help build a positive classroom culture and climate. The notion of *management* clearly translates to *control* and a certain role of the educators. While we do not want any classroom or school to be out of control, we acknowledge the importance of establishing structured and empowering strategies that encourage buy-in from all stakeholders in the classroom climate. With a positive climate, behaviors often will demonstrate those feelings as well.

- Days may be great and inspiring, and days may be draining—many times within the same 24 hours. In every chapter of this book, we share reminders and tips to help you thrive and survive. These first years are a lot of trial and error that help build a foundation for a solid career. Ride the highs of those successes while remembering not to sink too far into those lows.
- As you can see, we have taken risks in our careers that started with Day 1 for both of us. While those decisions were definitely not easy, we wouldn't be where we are today if we hadn't stepped out of our comfort zones to try new things.
- Kindness to yourself, compassion to the learners and families you serve, and collegiality with your fellow educators will keep you on the path to staying in this profession—with satisfaction and enthusiasm. This book shares ways that you may strive to understand others and yourself better as an educator to avoid burnout and to foster positive connections with those around you. Remember that you are human and (and your learners) begin fresh every day. The chapters about multilingual learners, avoiding a deficit mindset, and responsive learning remind us all about keeping the perspectives and experiences of the learners and families you serve at the forefront of everything you do.

You'll notice that there are stories and quotes shared by a variety of voices in education. We have novice teachers with under five years of experience who share current ideas of what is helping them find belonging and success in this profession. Veteran teachers reflect on things that they have learned over the years that they wish they knew earlier. Instructional coaches who are in and out of various classrooms daily discuss things that they see that are insightful and exciting. Administrators' perspectives on how to navigate your first years are included as well. Finally, there are some pieces shared by educators who speak from the points of view of family members and the unique points of view that we can appreciate and learn from. As we (Keri and Denise) have had diverse experiences in our journeys, we acknowledge that there are many more to share with you, and we sought to include those voices in this book.

While this book is crafted to have those critical conversations with our novice educators, we appreciate the veteran teachers who are taking their journeys alongside them. We see you, and we hope that this book reminds you of your incredible contributions to the lives you touch. We hope that the conversations you have with your colleagues continue to flourish as we all grow as educators.

Thank you for reading this book and allowing us to take this journey through your first years and beyond with you. We understand the calling that only education has for all of us, and we support you and we believe in you. You make a difference in people's lives daily, and children will look back at their time with you to reflect on things that they learned alongside you. You shape the future.

# DANGERS OF A DEFICIT MINDSET

CHAPTER 1

## Frontloaded Vocabulary

**deficit speech:** Language and thinking that classifies a particular group as being inadequate or deficient. This language often targets marginalized groups.

**asset-based language:** Language that focuses on the strengths, gifts, and talents of individuals and/or groups.

**learning loss:** The idea that due to a lapse in education due to certain experiences, such as COVID and virtual learning or summer break, students' learning has regressed.

**self-efficacy:** A person's belief in their ability to complete a task(s) that will influence change.

**teacher-efficacy:** Teachers' belief in their ability to positively impact students' lives and educational goals. ●

Who remembers *The Little Engine That Could*, by Watty Piper? As a child, it was my favorite book! I still have my copy from my childhood! It is the ultimate example of the power of positive thinking and how positive thinking can inspire achievement. "I think I can, I think I can, I think I can, I think I can." Because the Little Engine believed in its ability, it was able to overcome something thought to be insurmountable simply by repeating a positive affirmation. Imagine how powerful this tool could be if used with students daily.

Think back to March 2020, which was the beginning of many changes to the landscape of education. COVID-19 was the inspirer of ingenuity as educators formulated innovative ways to instruct our students in the virtual space. It was a difficult time for many. But somehow, our students found a way to be resilient, and they soon found their way back to the traditional classroom environment, which was not so traditional anymore. Things changed; our students changed, but their strength and resilience were apparent. Our students were success stories in so many ways. However, soon discussions about learning loss began to develop, and concerns about our students' academic growth—or lack thereof—began to become more pervasive. Despite being strong in the face of uncertainty during a challenging time, instead of focusing on the positives, the conversations turned toward the negatives. *Learning loss* became the prevalent language used when discussing our students. *Negative* or *deficit speech* became more dominant after the quarantine. Education professionals and other stakeholders began to talk about our students from a lens that was not positive, and we found ourselves reinvigorating the use of deficit thinking in education.

## What Is Deficit Thinking?

> *"Your mindset is your habit of thinking, your mental attitude about life. Attitudes are contagious. You are in a high stakes position where you are shaping minds. If you have a negative outlook on life, you are teaching impressionable minds to do the same."*
>
> —Donna, teacher and BOE member, Massachusetts

Deficit-thinking is rooted in biasness that places blame for subpar academic performance on marginalized and disenfranchised student populations (Fergus, 2022). It focuses on perceived shortcomings in certain groups that are cultural, and race based (Fergus, 2022). How many times have you heard a teacher say, "These kids can't learn" or "Nothing works. They just don't get it?" If you reflect on Donna's quote, she makes a valid point about how having a negative outlook can impact the students. However, this is not the first time we have encountered deficit speech. If we look at prior usage of the terminology, we will see that ideology of *learning loss* is preceded by similar deficit speech such as *achievement gap*, *at-risk*, *limited English proficiency*, and *summer decline*, all of which are directed at various cultural and lower socioeconomic groups while ignoring systems as solutions (Diamond et al., 2004; Gorski, 2011; Ladson-Billings, 2007; Lehman et al., 2021).

*"When my son had some difficulties in middle school, he was placed in a self-contained behavioral class to give him the support 'he needed' to find his way again. He knew immediately that the math in this course was way below his level and he asked quickly to leave the room for an inclusion setting—and received a lot of resistance from teachers and administrators. He moved and did well in the class. He then asked to leave the self-contained room for science. The teacher laughed in his face and laughed in my face as well. She said no student from their class has ever been successful in that class because there is so much group work. Well, he moved into the science course and earned a 100 each marking period. When I asked if he succeeded just to spite the people that thought he couldn't do it, he laughed and replied, 'Absolutely!'"*

—Rose, parent

## LABELS

*"I heard all types of educators call students 'low' right in front of them or detail the things they think the student 'can't' do. I think people think they are sharing information that is helpful, but that type of label is never going to benefit a student—whether or not they are there to hear someone say it."*

—Denise, ML educator and author

When one considers ways that we refer to learners, sometimes the labels that we use highlight things about children that are not their strengths. Historically, the names that the field of education has used to identify subgroups of learners have been used to delineate diverse groups from learners who are the "norm."

As educators, we find that labeling students can be problematic because it puts the students in categories that enable the people around them to view them in a singular lens. For example, let's discuss students who are labeled as "gifted." There is an expectation that these students are going to excel regardless of circumstances. But we must remember that our students are still children. Thus, they will have moments when they are not performing well. Should they then be subjected to comments such as "I know you can do better than that" or "You are in these classes for a reason. Do you want to risk not being in gifted classes anymore?" These types of comments don't consider what the underlying issues may be. Is the student struggling and uncertain how to ask for assistance? Are there issues at home? Teachers who fall into this trap can begin to adopt a negative mindset that can be potentially dangerous to the student if they don't know how to verbalize or compartmentalize their thoughts and feelings. No student is safe from a deficit mindset or deficit-based speech, no matter how they are categorized, as long as educators continue to experience and express negative thoughts about them.

There has been a movement in various areas in education to intentionally move away from negative jargon. Administrators in particular need to challenge all staff to use positive language when describing students. Educators should begin with the positives and then move on to offering assistance and comprehension of what the student needs.

> *"This student is so low."*
>
> *"This student is a behavior kid."*
>
> *"Those parents aren't involved."*
>
> *"I've been told a LOT of really deficit-driven statements like the ones above. And—to be honest—I've also SAID a lot of deficit-driven statements like these as well. It is only within reflective conversations, lots of a-ha moments, and tons of professional growth that I've realized how problematic a lot of these statements are—and now that I know better, I do better. I'm constantly calling myself out for my own language choices. I'm constantly reflecting and becoming more and more aware of my own biases (we all have them!)."*
>
> —Carly, ML/EL specialist, Illinois

Can we give Carly a round of applause?! How many teachers have that moment of self-realization and notice that they use deficit speech often? Teachers are indoctrinated into a culture that is rife with negative speech. Education is a profession where the conversation is often centered around how students are failing, teachers are failing, and how "no child should be left behind." When teachers are blamed for their students' learning deficits, the default language or thought becomes "These children can't learn" or "I give up."

To avoid using deficit speech, it is good to identify language that would be deemed negative. Table 1.1 is a suggested list of language and ideas to avoid when discussing your student population.

**Table 1.1**

## Language to Avoid When Discussing Your Student Population

| DEFICIT TERM | WHY IT'S HARMFUL | ASSET-BASED TERM | WHY IT'S BETTER |
|---|---|---|---|
| Clustering: grouping students based on similar learning needs | Reinforces stereotypes and can highlight inequities | Flexible grouping | Focuses on addressing various learning needs |
| Tracking | Focuses on students with deficits and limits | Student goal setting | Focuses on the positive aspects of student achievement |
| Ability-grouping | Groupings are focused on deficits rather than strengths | Flexible grouping | Focuses on addressing various learning needs |
| Intervention kids | Labels and categorizes students based on challenges and deficits | Students receiving support | Reinforces strengths and does not focus on a particular group |
| Inclusion classroom | Implies that it is not a standard classroom environment | Supportive or diverse learners classroom | Suggest that all learners require support based on diverse learning needs |
| Inclusion program | Focuses on the disability of the students | Universal support program | Encompasses all students and does not single out one group of students |
| Inclusion kids | Focuses on the disability of the students | Students receiving support | Suggest that all learners require support based on diverse learning needs |
| Subgroups | Separates students based on deficits | Collaborative learning groups | Suggests that students work together without the idea of labeling being present |

*(Continued)*

(Continued)

| DEFICIT TERM | WHY IT'S HARMFUL | ASSET-BASED TERM | WHY IT'S BETTER |
|---|---|---|---|
| Monolinguals/ Bilinguals | Can nurture stereotypes | Multilingual learners | Implies that being able to speak multiple languages is a positive skill |
| At-risk students | Labels students based on deficits and ability | Students needing support | This does not single out a particular group of students |
| Minority | Implies that a group is lesser than other groups | diverse | Differences are positive |
| Pull-out | Students are being removed from classroom and singled out based on deficits | Students receiving support | This does not single out a particular group of students; any student can receive support |
| Push-in | Singles out students in the classroom environment based on deficits | Collaborative teaching | Teachers are working in tandem to support all students without singling out one particular group |
| Transition or transient students | Suggests that there are deficits due to inconsistency or instability | Newcomers or incoming students | Does not label students based on mobility |
| Illegals | Implies that students are criminals or not legally in the country | Mixed immigration status | Does not specify the exact status of the student |

What a list!! Any language that labels students in a way that can be thought of in a negative sense should be avoided. Changing the mindset may be difficult because as educators, we have been indoctrinated into this thought process. However, if we want to inspire our students, we need to think from an asset-based lens and not from a deficit-based lens. There are ways to create an environment conducive to implementing practices where asset-based speech is the preferred speech when referring to students.

- Create a list of terms that teachers can use when having meetings about students. This list should be used during team meetings, meetings with parents, or any meetings where students will be discussed.

- To counter, create a list of terms that teachers should not use when referring to students in team meetings, meetings with parents, or any meetings where students will be discussed.
- When interacting with students, use asset-based speech when discussing behavior, academic achievement, and social-emotional or other issues. Students appreciate positive dialogue, so engage them using positive and asset-based speech.

There will be situations when a colleague or peer continues to use deficit speech when referring to our students. Seek to redirect your colleagues in a positive manner as well. For example, it is a good idea to start meetings by reviewing meeting protocols relative to using asset-based speech. It is also acceptable to redirect in a respectful way by making a statement such as, "Is there another way for us to discuss the student using asset-based language?" It is a culture shift—but one that can positively impact students and staff alike.

## Reframing Learning Loss

Let's ponder what we call the illusion of learning loss. Students experienced trauma-induced teaching and learning during the COVID crisis. Learning virtually was challenging for students because the virtual world can be isolating and students do not get to access or develop social skills they would access by working with classmates and their teachers. But who said they lost anything?

Test data has always been used to substantiate the thought that there is learning gains and/or loss, and this was highlighted even more when students were subject to learning online during the pandemic. Because students were learning in a nontraditional sense, educators need to reimagine traditional and standardized testing methods post-COVID, as they may be unfair measures of their learning and skills.

Assessment needs to focus on students' strengths and using those strengths to engage students and let them share their learning with you. Asset-based assessment, letting students have a voice in sharing with their teachers and stakeholders what they have learned, is the way forward. Classroom teachers can give varied assessments to address learning needs and styles. They are the true gauge of whether a student has gained or "lost," because they have access to varied data and they have knowledge of our students' needs, which is something to ponder and to discuss in the chapter, Grading and Assessments.

What is often not highlighted is what students *gained* post-COVID and what they continue to gain that negates the notion of deficit thinking. While a student may have struggled academically, there are other areas where students may have excelled. For example, COVID largely forced students to begin taking part in their learning. Many teachers likely saw that students would meet outside of virtual class to do work and projects. Students formed their own groups or asked to be put into breakout rooms to work with their classmates to collaborate in projects or just for the sake of socializing. They found their strengths and would use those positives to contribute to the group. This was a source of pride for students. Students did not *lose*, but they *gained* independence, resiliency, creativity, communication skills, and more. The intangible skills are valuable and helped students greatly. Students are able to voice these gains, too!! When working with students on Jamboard, a digital bulletin board platform, students discussed some of the intangibles that they took away from their experience with COVID and online learning:

- "I've learned how to be patient."
- "I should ask for help when I need it."
- "I learned that your work doesn't have to be finished in time."
- "I've learned to love myself."

Students did not mention academics, but what is mentioned is positive and evidence of the resiliency of our students. In addition, they used asset-based speech to voice their thoughts.

## From Deficit to Asset-Based Communication

> *"There will always be some students that struggle academically more than others. It is important as educators to see each student as an individual in order to meet his or her needs. All students have the ability to learn and progress despite the adversities they may be facing in their personal lives. High expectations must be held for all students."*
>
> —Trish, educator, New Jersey

Trish's statement is true. Educators must see students as individuals. It is import because they *all* have needs. Eliminating the use of deficit speech increases teachers' sense of efficacy. Teacher efficacy is derived from self-efficacy, which is defined as "teachers' belief in their judgments about their capability to influence and encourage student learning" (Hoy & Spero, 2005; Orange, 2018). If teachers increase their usage of asset-based language and indoctrinate their students into a culture of positive thinking, student success will result in teachers potentially experiencing an increased sense of efficacy. Teachers can create an environment that is conducive to positive and asset-based speech. Some ideas include the following:

- Give students choice when it comes to assessment. If students are assessed in a way that addresses their strengths, they may do well and experience success, thus increasing their self-esteem.
- Have a word wall with alternative positive words and phrases that students can use instead of deficit-based speech. In addition, teachers will use the word wall with the students when having conversations in the classroom. This word wall will have encouraging words and phrases as well as speech the teacher can use when reviewing work with students in small groups or during one-on-one conferences.
- When talking to colleagues about students, use asset-based speech. Students hear everything. Teachers should not have conversations about students in a public space. However, if that transpires, using asset-based speech is necessary. Also, while in grade-level team meetings, teachers should use asset-based language so that they develop a culture of positivity not negativity.
- Poll students and ask them what you can do to create a positive environment. Students know what they want and need to feel encouraged and supported in an academic space. Giving students voice always lends itself to instilling positivity in the students.

## PARENTS, FAMILIES, AND COMMUNITY COMMUNICATION

Something else to consider when we think of deficit speech and changing the narrative into something asset based is indoctrinating the school community into the mindset of using asset-based language. When teachers are engaging with parents, it is important to operate from a positive lens. For example, when meeting with parents, if there are concerns about a student's academic, social, or emotional growth, frame the language from a positive scope. Parents are invested in their children and want to see their children succeed. However, there may be bumps on the road to success. It is alright to identify the issues, because parents need to know how they can support their children in the academic space. But instead of saying, "Your child can't . . .", how about saying, "Your child needs support with. . . ." See Table 1.2 for further suggestions.

**Table 1.2**

## Suggestions for Replacing Deficit-Based Speech With Asset-Based Speech

| DON'T SAY THIS (DEFICIT-BASED SPEECH) | SAY THIS (ASSET-BASED SPEECH) |
|---|---|
| Your child can't . . . . | Your child needs support in this area. |
| Their behavior in class is not good. | Can you give me suggestions on how to connect with your child? |
| They do not pay attention in class. | What are some ways I can inspire your child to focus during instruction? |
| Your child is failing. | Your child needs additional support in this content area. |

These are just some examples of using positive speech when engaging parents. Parents are more comfortable when they hear a teacher positively engage with them and may be receptive to receiving information that may not be positive. It is all about how you frame the conversation. In addition, parents may reciprocate and use asset-based speech when meeting with teachers, especially when they recognize that a teacher is operating in the best interest of their child. We must always remember that educating the whole child is a team effort. Everyone must engage in a healthy and constructive way, because the goal is to ensure that the needs of the child are met.

## Conclusion

It is important to remember to think before you speak because students listen even when you think that they aren't listening. Speak encouragement into your students because they will benefit academically, socially, and emotionally. Use affirmative dialogue when engaging parents because they will support you in all your endeavors as an educator. You will find that those positive words are meaningful and impactful and can invigorate the learning environment for all stakeholders, including *yourself*!

## DISCUSSION QUESTIONS

- What is *deficit thinking* in the educational environment?
- Think about situations in which you have experienced deficit thinking in the classroom or educational environment. Journal or share examples of your experiences.
- How does deficit thinking impact students in the classroom and the educational environment?
- How can educators adopt an asset-based mindset? How can asset-based language be used in the classroom? ●

# UNDERSTANDING AND SURVIVING THE EVALUATION

CHAPTER

2

## Frontloaded Vocabulary

**corrective action plan (CAP):** An education plan used to address any teacher performance issues or negative evaluations during the school year.

**differentiate:** Tailoring instruction to meet the needs of the diverse student population in your classroom.

**teacher-speak:** Teacher language used during instruction. Some examples include "1-2-3, eyes on me."

**student-speak:** Language that students use when working with each other or with the teacher.

**Individual Education Plan (IEP):** An education plan for students who were screened by the Child Study Team and qualify for special services.

**504:** An education plan for students who do not qualify for special services but require modifications, such as extra time on assessments, FM systems and amplifiers, or other accommodation.

**multilingual learner:** Students who are learning in a language other than their native language.

**project-based learning (PBL):** Instructional approach that engages students in hands-on projects. These projects can be used as assessment tools and allow students to exhibit their strengths and talents.

*(Continued)*

**formative assessment:** Assessment that occurs during instruction. Some examples include Turn and Talk, sticky note check-ins, polls, Q&A, quizzes, games, journaling.

**summative assessment:** Assessment that occurs at the end of a unit. Some examples include unit test, project, essay. ●

Twice a year, teachers are visited by their building administrators or content area supervisors. If you are a novice teacher, those visits are more frequent and unannounced, causing feelings of anxiety or stress. Why? When students are involved, one never knows what may transpire because students bring with them a plethora of issues to unpack daily. One may experience a great lesson while your administrator is present, or everything can go up in flames like a dumpster fire. The teacher evaluation process is one thing that can make any teacher, novice or veteran, sigh deeply and hope for the best! In this chapter, we will discuss the evaluation process in detail.

## Why Are Evaluations Conducted?

Students are regularly assessed by their classroom teachers and given assessments by the state to ensure they meet standards and criteria for learning. In that same vein, the purpose of teacher evaluation is to assess teacher effectiveness and is an opportunity to give teachers constructive feedback that can positively influence their teacher practice. Further, teacher evaluation is necessary because teaching and learning are intertwined, and for that connection to be maximized, we should document the quality of teacher performance (Stronge, 2006). Teacher evaluation should not be a punitive tool, although some teachers see it as such. When effectively used, teacher evaluation is a prescriptive tool, used to give teachers prescribed suggestions on how to hone their craft and assist improving their teacher practice. In addition, it should be viewed as a growth model because educators are always learning, evolving, and *growing* in their craft. Education is a career that necessitates having individuals who are willing to continually develop and amend their skills to meet the needs of the students they teach. Teachers and administrators dialogue about planning and implementing lessons that are engaging and inspire learning in the classroom. Further, conversations about the student population and how to meet their needs are also a topic that is discussed during evaluation conferences. In addition, discussions about the many facets of teaching are had because of teacher evaluation. For example, teachers may discuss assessment tools that can be used to meet the needs of the diverse classroom population.

Or teachers may ask for advice about classroom management techniques when dealing with challenging students. When used constructively, the evaluation process can yield positive results and improve teacher practice at all levels.

There are many teacher evaluation tools adopted by school districts to assess teacher effectiveness. However, no matter the tool used, these evaluation tools have common criteria that are useful to teacher practice. For example, an evaluative tool should include but is not limited to the following:

- Lesson planning and preparation
- Classroom management
- Professionalism and conduct
- Student engagement

No matter what tool a district uses, these items are the common thread and the focus of the evaluation process. As we dig deeper into these components, let's ponder and review the process.

## The Evaluation Process

To maximize comprehension of the positive aspects of the evaluation process, it is important to understand the steps involved.

### STEP 1: PRE-OBSERVATION MEETING

This is the time when the teacher meets with the administrator or supervisor who is conducting the evaluation. Prior to the pre-observation meeting, you will be tasked with completing a pre-observation form that provides the evaluator with the lesson plan and an idea of what the teacher and students will be doing during the lesson. In addition, some evaluation models include pre-observation questions about the students in the classroom. Teachers include information about the number of students in the classroom and their abilities. When the teacher and evaluator briefly meet prior to the observation, the pre-observation documents, including the lesson plan, presentation slides, and any documents to be used during the lesson, are shared and reviewed. If there are any questions, comments, or concerns about lesson implementation, dialogue should take place. Oftentimes, the evaluator will give feedback about lesson components, such as the learning activities or assessment. For example, the evaluator may ask the teacher how they intend to assess the needs of the learners in the classroom or inquire about how a paraprofessional might be used during a lesson. Novice teachers should take the opportunity to listen and reevaluate lesson activities based on any feedback that the evaluator may share. However, the pre-observation conference is beneficial to all teachers and should be viewed as a chance to reevaluate a lesson.

To reiterate, here are components of the pre-observation conference:

- Begin with a discussion of the curriculum and scope and sequence of the lesson.
- What are the demographics of the classroom: Are there students with IEPs, 504s, MLs, or other?
- What modifications, if necessary, will be put in place for students during the lesson?
- What are the objectives and learning outcomes of the lesson?
- How will you engage the students during the lesson? Think "I Do, We Do, You Do" lesson format.
- How will you differentiate instruction for the students?
- What assessment practices are included in your lesson?

## STEP 2: THE OBSERVATION

Show time!! The observation is when the teacher gets to show their skills to the evaluator. Be prepared for any and everything to potentially go wrong!! However, even if there is a misstep, technology glitch, or some other mishap, those negatives can easily become positives because it allows you to monitor and adjust your lesson as needed. Flexibility is an important skill to exhibit in the classroom environment, and most evaluators want to see teachers think fast on their feet! There could be an emergency drill or some other event that could disrupt the lesson during the observation. How you react and adjust are also focal points to the lesson. Thus, be prepared to adapt by having backup activities and being flexible, because you never know what may occur. Administrators will be looking out for three key markers: student engagement, peer-to-peer interaction, and assessment methodology.

### *1. Engage the students*

This is possibly one of the most difficult parts of the observation. Students are a captive audience, because they have no choice in how information is delivered to them. Teachers follow the curriculum and create lessons, but traditionally, students have no voice when it comes to how instruction is delivered. Thus, it is important to have knowledge of student interests to plan introductory activities that engage the students and pique their curiosity. When you think about your student population, getting to know your students goes beyond ability. You want to gauge their interests and use that information to make instruction accessible to the students in your midst. There are several things that you can do that can engage students:

- Using a song to introduce a lesson. Music is a unifier, and I have used songs to "pump up the crowd" and prepare students for instruction.
- Taking a poll. When I was in the classroom, at the beginning of a lesson, I would take a poll using Poll Everywhere or Mentimeter. This way when we reviewed the answers, students could share their thoughts without being put on the spot. You can also take a poll to tap prior knowledge.
- Playing a game, like *Kahoot* or *Quizlet*, is another way to engage the students. The game can be used as a preassessment, and at the end of the lesson, the information can be revisited.
- Analyzing a picture that is related to the lesson. I taught social studies, and we used to use pictures to analyze and discuss what the students thought was happening in the picture. This is something that can also be done in other content areas, allowing students to make predictions. Using pictures also addresses the needs of your visual learners and your multilingual learners who use pictures to nurture understanding.
- Asking a question and having students Turn and Talk to their partners of tablemates. Peer learning is beneficial to students. I often say there is "teacher-speak" and "student-speak." I could explain something in "teacher-speak," but there were always those students who could better explain to their peers using "student-speak."

### 2. Notice students interacting with each other

Peer-to-peer learning is one of the best ways to engage students. When students do partner work, they learn how to communicate and socialize with each other. Socialization is significant because we are in the digital age when our youth communicate in the cyberverse. Thus, human-to-human interaction is important to nurture as our students prepare for the future. In addition, problem-solving skills are enhanced when students work on projects together. Students will contribute their knowledge and skills to partner and/or group work, building self-esteem and encouraging their peers. Students who are withdrawn or shy will find their voice when working with their peers because they feel as though they are safe with their classmates. They take risks when working with their classmates that they may not otherwise take. I enjoy watching students interact with each other when doing classwork. You get to witness students blossoming when they interact with each other!

### 3. Use various methods of assessment

During a lesson, teachers must gauge student understanding of concepts. There is a plethora of ways that one can do this during the lesson. Here are a few suggestions:

- Turn and Talk
- Taking a poll
- Using games
- Engaging the students in group discussion
- Project-based learning

These are just a few of the assessment tools that an educator can used during the evaluation. What is imperative is that you use an assessment tool that will allow you to ascertain what the students learned and what you need to reteach. While it is important to use an assessment that is student friendly, you also want to gather useful data that will drive future instruction.

The observation is not a process to fear. Think of it as having company over for dinner and you want to serve your best dish. Some may enjoy it; others may not. But it is an opportunity to show your skills. Embrace the moment and grow from it!

## STEP 3: POST-OBSERVATION MEETING

The post-observation meeting is very important to the evaluative process. During this meeting, the teacher is allowed to self-reflect and offer insights about how they could improve the lesson or how effective the lesson was. *Always* take the time to self-reflect because that is the only way teacher practice can improve. Be prepared to share thoughts about your performance and assess the effectiveness of the lesson. After the administrator or evaluator offers feedback, it is important to use that feedback to drive future instruction. When discussing the suggestions being made by the evaluator, ask for assistance with enacting the suggestions that were given. Your principal or supervisor will offer guidance or point you in the direction of where to find information that will assist you. That could be a professional development opportunity or suggesting a mentor to assist you. If the feedback is negative and a corrective action plan (CAP) is needed, work in conjunction with the evaluator to set attainable goals to assist with improving practice. Also take the time to consider the following when self-reflecting on the lesson:

- Consider if the students learned what you intended. Study exit tickets or other evaluative methods used at the conclusion of the lesson to ascertain what students learned and what you may have to revisit in the future. That information will assist you when planning the next lesson or units of instruction.
- How would you teach the lesson in the future? This a question often asked during the post-observation meeting, and it is one that teachers should seriously consider. You may want to teach the lesson again. Thus, it is important to consider what worked and what did not. There is no such thing as a perfect lesson, *but* there are parts of every lesson that are effective. Once I taught a math lesson on fractions using skittles. Students had the same total amount of Skittles, but the number of each color Skittle was different for each group. For example, each group had 12 Skittles, but one group may have had 2 red, 3 green, 1 yellow, 4 orange, and 2 purple, while another group had 4 red, 2 green, 2 yellow, 3 orange, and 1 purple. When it was time to analyze data, it was difficult for all students to be on the same page because each group had different fractions. Since that was the first lesson, it would have been more effective for students to have the same number of Skittles, including the same number of each color. As an extension activity, I could have created an evaluation tool by giving students a different number of each color of Skittles to test mastery.
- Did you address the needs of all the learners in your classroom, and if so, were the modifications and adjustments successful? During your reflection, you must consider the tools used to address the needs of students in your class, such as those with IEPs, 504s, or students who are multilingual learners. In addition, you want to consider what other needs students may have because they bring so much to the classroom. Being hungry, having personal difficulties, emotional traumas, and other situations affect your students. This is information that will prove useful when teaching. Ultimately, your goal, as an educator, is to fill your teacher toolbox with activities that will assist you with instruction and with reaching all your learners!

## Lesson Planning: The Good, Bad, and Sometimes Ugly

One of the most important parts of the evaluation process is the lesson plan, the blueprint for what you will be teaching during the observation. Lesson plans are sometimes the bane of an educator's existence. They serve as a roadmap or outline that guides instruction. During the evaluation process, the evaluator will request and review the lesson plan, so it is important to include the necessary information when sharing. What are the most important parts of lesson plans and how can they guide you when you are being evaluated by building administrators and supervisors?

## SETTING OBJECTIVES

When writing lesson plans, it is important to write objectives that focus on what students will *learn* rather than what they will *do*. The activities are important; however, the learning objective is more important. The activities are just a means to an end. Incorporating the SMART (specific, measurable, achievable, relevant, and time-bound) criteria assists when setting objectives.

- **Planning activities:** Engagement! That is the key here! Student engagement is paramount because evaluators want to see that students are engaged in the learning. Including diverse activities ensures that student needs are being met. Students have varied learning styles and interests. Thus, it is important to plan a myriad of activities that will engage all the learners in your classroom.
- **Differentiation of instruction:** This speaks to the prior point of planning activities. Not only will there be students with varied learning styles in the classroom, but there will also be students with varied learning needs and abilities. Classroom populations can include students who are gifted or students with IEPs and 504s. Thus, differentiation of instruction must occur so that the teacher can impact and maximize student engagement and learning.
- **Assessing student learning:** In every evaluation meeting, teachers are asked, "How will you know that the students have learned what you wanted them to learn?" Assessment is important because it also gauges effectiveness, not necessarily teacher effectiveness but lesson effectiveness. Did the teacher plan activities that were engaging and allowed students to meet the lesson objectives? In another chapter, Grading and Assessment, we will discuss assessment further. But it is important to include varied types of assessment to meet the needs of varied learners. Formative and summative assessments can be used simultaneously and effectively to gauge student learning. Short quizzes or taking polls during a lesson will let the teacher know that the students are engaged and accessing the content. Project-based learning projects are also a great way to allow students to use their skills to create something that not only addresses their learning needs but also showcases varied talents and skills.

What is the "ugly" part of lesson plans? They can be time consuming, especially when writing a lengthy unit plan. However, having the blueprint to guide instruction is like having a map to guide you to your destination. Sometimes you may take the wrong road, but if you reach your destination, even if you go in another direction, having the map or guide assist you is important!

## TEACHER REFLECTION

Did the students learn what you wanted them to learn?! That is always the question evaluators ask after a teacher evaluation. *But* just as important is did *you* learn anything because of the evaluation? What are your takeaways from the feedback received from the evaluator? Teacher reflection is just as important as student learning. Self-evaluation is significant because teachers should make judgments and acknowledge their knowledge, beliefs, and performance (Stronge, 2006). Feedback, positive or negative, can be impactful to teacher practice, and using that feedback to drive future practice is valuable (see Table 2.1).

**Table 2.1**

### The Dos and Don'ts of Feedback

| DO | DON'T |
|---|---|
| Use the feedback given to you by the evaluators. Ask how you can improve your practice. | View the feedback as negative. There is always something positive to be taken from any type of feedback. |
| Ask your colleagues and peers to review any feedback with you. Seek out veteran teachers to assist with improving your practice. Try to co-plan with teachers during PLC meetings or some other collaborative planning time. | Turn away offers from your colleagues to assist you with improving your practice. During preparation periods, go observe veteran teachers during their instructional time. |
| Get feedback from your students. You can take a poll or use a Google Form exit ticket to ask students to give you feedback about your lesson. They are your target audience, and they will give you insight into how effective you are! | Personalize feedback from the students. Yes, they can give insight, but remember, they are children in some cases and may not know how to effectively share their thoughts. Don't adopt the "They don't like me" train of thought. |
| Seek out professional development opportunities that will help you improve in the areas identified by your evaluator(s) as needing improvement. | Give up. Teacher practice is ever evolving. There is no such thing as perfection when in education, but there is such a thing as *growth*, and as educators, we grow and evolve every day!! |

## Conclusion

Teacher evaluation is an essential component of professional improvement for educators. Ensuring understanding of the process as well as using feedback can positively impact future practice. In addition, remember that lesson planning is an important element of the evaluation process, and embrace using this instructional blueprint as you continue to seek ways to educate students in an engaging way.

## DISCUSSION QUESTIONS

- What is the evaluation process, and why is it significant to professional growth?
- How can feedback be used to improve practice?
- What issues may arise from an unsatisfactory evaluation, and how can teachers self-advocate constructively?

CHAPTER

3

# GRADING AND ASSESSMENTS/ PROJECT-BASED LEARNING

## Frontloaded Vocabulary

**assessment:** Evaluating, measuring, and documenting student learning and growth; assessment gauges strengths and weaknesses and informs instruction.

**project-based learning (PBL):** Using projects to gathering evidence of student learning and performance. Critical thinking, collaboration, communication, and creativity are crucial parts of PBLs.

**flow theory:** A concept first coined by psychologist Mihaly Csikszentmihalyi, who noticed that when someone is hyper-focused and completely engaged in their work, engagement is boosted significantly. ●

## What Is Assessment, and Why Is It Important?

Quiz. Test. Assessment. These are some of the words that conjure feelings of dread and frustration, not only for the students but also for educators. Assessment is part of the teaching and learning process, because teachers need to gauge student learning. Useful data can be gathered from assessments given to students.

However, educators must be mindful of how to assess the diverse learners in our midst. Teachers are constantly told to differentiate instruction; thus, it would make sense to give students an assessment that is differentiated as opposed to one that is common and one note. By assessing students in a way that differs from how they were taught, they are being set up for test anxiety and failure. This is not the goal of assessment and this will not yield useful data.

The purpose of assessments is critical for all educators to understand. In the field of education, assessments are the diverse methods or tools used to evaluate, measure, and document the academic readiness, learning progress, skill acquisition, or educational needs of students (Williams, 2011). Many different types of assessments serve a variety of goals for our students (see Table 3.1).

**Table 3.1**

## Types of Assessments

| TYPE | DEFINITION | PURPOSE | WHEN THEY'RE USED |
|---|---|---|---|
| Formative assessments | Tests, quizzes, projects, and other assignments that teachers use to determine *next steps* in instruction. May be formal or informal and sometimes may be teacher-created. | To inform what students know and what they need more reinforcement with. *This is what your students demonstrate that they have learned and what they need to learn in future lessons.* | In every lesson, whether they are exit slips/tickets where students share what they learned, anecdotal notes students may keep while reading texts or via observations and notations by the teacher. |
| Summative assessments | Assessments at the end of the unit, chapter, year, or lesson. These are more often formal and connected specifically to grade-level curriculum. | The goal is to already know what learners have mastered or understood before we get to the summative assessments. *This is what your students demonstrate that they have learned in this unit but this does not necessarily inform what they need to learn in future lessons.* | Often used as *culminating assessments* as students complete a topic or skill. |

| TYPE | DEFINITION | PURPOSE | WHEN THEY'RE USED |
|---|---|---|---|
| Diagnostic assessments | Skills-based assessments, evaluations for additional educational services, and other district-level assessment. | To determine academic levels or other educational needs. *These assessments give information that is useful for placement and measurement of student needs.* | In response to a concern (testing for eligibility for special programs) or to provide needed information to design pathways for education for learners. |
| Standardized assessments | Annual tests in certain and formal assessments that are graduation requirements. | Considered to be *high-stakes assessments* as a learner's academic future may depend on the results. *High-stakes assessments are often used as measures of aptitude that determine eligibility for graduation or other programs.* | Required assessments at the state or federal level that are normed with students in the same grade level. |
| Benchmark assessments | Assessments such as intelligence tests and assessments given at the district level that compare students to others considered their peers in which the data is analyzed at both a local level and on a broad scale. | Designed to measure growth on similar assessments. *Benchmarking assessments take a broad view that allows you to see trends or movements.* | Given at different parts of the school year to supply educators and stakeholders with benchmark data. |

*"There are many things about standardized tests that I have felt to be unfair to learners with diverse needs. In fact, I have advocated for fewer assessments like these that may categorize our learners in a way that puts roadblocks in their paths. With that being said, when we did not have the information from these tests during the pandemic, I did find that I had use for some of the information that we glean from the results."*

—Denise, ML educator and author

> *"I understand and appreciate the importance of collecting data through assessments. When results of tests or evaluations are used in a way that informs instruction or shows gaps in student knowledge, this is useful only when there are actionable plans for analyzing that information and making plans to support students in these areas."*
>
> —Anna

## Common Assessment Fallacies

When we think of assessment and what it looks like, there are many who envision assessment in a "traditional" sense. There is the ever-reliable multiple-choice test that we still see on standardized assessments. Educators also use fill-in-the-blank, true-or-false questions, and matching. These types of questions have been used for years, and in some classrooms, you will still find these questions on quizzes and tests. Questions such as these are problematic for several reasons.

1. Multiple-choice questions can often lead to confusion if they are not constructed correctly. For example, in some instances, students have been led to believe that more than one option could be the potential answer. This confuses students and can cause major anxiety in test takers.
2. Fill-in-the-blank questions and matching questions can also lead to confusion if students struggle with vocabulary. In addition, there can also be several options, and these types of questions can also confuse test takers.
3. These kinds of questions do not test skill or application. To truly assess students' comprehension of a concept, creating and using questions that allow students to analyze and apply what they have learned are better gauges of student knowledge.

Assessment in any form is necessary to verify student proficiency. The types of questions mentioned may be effective for formative assessment. However, it is important that assessment shows application of skills. Assessment doesn't have to be cookie cutter and boring.

The question all educators should be asking themselves is, how can we assess students in a fun and engaging way *and* collect data that allows us to gauge student strengths and weaknesses?

## What Assessment Should Look Like

Educators have a great deal of control when it comes to formulating assessments. Classroom teachers are on the frontline doing the work with the students and have access to information that allows them to create assessments that address the needs of the diverse learners in their midst. Teacher autonomy is often frowned upon; however, when it comes to knowing what is best for their students and how to teach and assess them, teacher autonomy is a powerful tool. Having the ability to take control of one's own teaching means having the control to assess that teaching in a modality that is engaging and student centered. Teachers should feel empowered to poll the students and ask them about their individual strengths and weaknesses, their likes and dislikes, and their talents. This can be done in person or digitally by using a Google Form, for example. Most important, educators should ask students how they would like to be assessed, if they were given the opportunity to choose. We will discuss polling and surveys later in the chapter.

In my years as a classroom educator, after polling my students year after year, here are some of the most frequent responses and requests around assessment, directly from students:

1. Assessment should be fun. If students have to take a test or be assessed, they want to enjoy doing it. If learners feel engaged in these activities, they will be motivated to put effort into their work.
2. Assessment choice is critical. Choice means voice. Learners want to have a say in what the assessment is and they want to have a voice in how they are to be graded. They can also assist with creating rubrics and other tools for grading. Learners are then stakeholders in both the validity of the assessments and their own learning.
3. Assessment that addresses their various learning needs and styles allows learners to empower themselves and recognize ways that they are talented or confident. If you are artistically talented, how can you be assessed using your strengths and not your weaknesses?

## The Problem With Assessment

Differentiated instruction. Multiple intelligences. Various learning styles and abilities. IEPs. 504s. Giftedness. Why are we discussing these items? These are all things that affect teaching. Thus, it should affect assessment. Teachers are constantly reminded to address students' learning styles and differentiate their instruction. It is imperative that IEPs and 504s are reviewed and implemented. It is the responsibility of the teacher to ensure that when delivering instruction, these guidelines are adhered to. *But* when teachers are differentiating instruction and addressing learners' needs, assessment does not necessarily address these needs. This is especially true when we look at standardized tests that are not differentiated at all! Students with IEPs and 504s may receive extra time and accommodations; however, they *still* take the same test as everyone else. How are students expected to *pass* a test that is not differentiated or designed to meet their specific learning needs? How is that a fair or accurate assessment of student knowledge? We will discuss IEPs and 504 plans in more detail in Chapter 6.

Let's take this a step further. Equity and access. . . . Many times, our children are exposed to assessment language that betrays their knowledge. For example, I had a young student taking a test (NJASK or New Jersey Assessment of Skills and Knowledge, at the time), and the word *yacht* was on the test. When the student asked what it meant, I could not provide assistance. The student had a complete meltdown because of her unfamiliarity with the word. Students come from all walks of life. Not all students have the same opportunities or level of exposure due to differences in socioeconomic status, language barriers, or access to technology. How many students know what a *yacht* is? Many have not seen a yacht or a boat. Further, the spelling is confusing, so a student might have difficulty even understanding the pronunciation of the word in order to say it and know what it means.

Thus, assessment does not address learning needs. Assessment does not address exposure or socioeconomic status. Assessment does not address abilities. Assessment, in many instances, is one size fits all, especially standardized assessments. You must ask why educators are being told to differentiate instruction and are being evaluated on how they differentiate instruction, but students are not given a differentiated assessment, especially at the state level. Furthermore, teachers are evaluated based on standardized tests, *but* it is an unfair evaluation because students are given an assessment that doesn't reflect the type of instruction teachers have been directed to give. It is a vicious cycle, one that diminishes teachers' sense of efficacy. There has to be a better way to assess students *and* gauge teacher effectiveness using an assessment modality that matches how teachers are giving instruction to how students are assessed. How can we make that a reality?! By examining our assessment practices, the beginnings of creating and implementing equitable assessment for our students focused on assessing what is taught in a meaningful way can be beneficial to our students (Brown, 2021). Dorroh (2019) wrote about giving his students the opportunity to choose how they were assessed in science class. He found that students were immersed in the learning process, and by choosing an assessment modality they enjoyed, student engagement and mastery of content was high. Let's dig deeper into the benefits of allowing student choice in assessment.

## The Benefits of Allowing Choice in Assessment

We all have confidence in different areas. Some learners are excellent in writing essays or long-answer responses. Other learners prefer to design something that shows mastery of a concept. Still others feel confident that they can present the required information orally either in an in-person presentation or in a recorded video. All may be excellent ways for learners to show mastery or understanding of a topic in a way that plays to their strengths.

> *"Providing different ways in which our students can demonstrate understanding or mastery is a great way to give access to the content. When students know that they have choices in how they show what they know, they feel empowered and engaged. I have personally used menu boards to allow students to work to their strengths with great results. As part of the 'main dish' component, some students chose to create 3D models, others chose to produce really complex videos, and yet others made incredible Google Slides presentations. 'Appetizers' and 'desserts' provided more structured activities that set up the foundations of the vocabulary or basic concepts of the unit. These types of assessments are always a hit and they authentically allow students to demonstrate what they have learned in ways that specifically address the curriculum."*
>
> —Joseph

Offering differentiation when assessing students grabs the students' attention and enables them to connect with the material rather than just studying for a quiz or test (Davenport, 2018). If learners feel a sense of agency and control over at least some aspects of how they demonstrate their progress or mastery, they will take a role in their own learning and reflection—which is often more important than the things that are being assessed. We strive to establish the goal of becoming lifelong, reflective learners. Portfolios are also great ways to engage learners while giving them space to review their own work and select samples that best represent their strengths. Digital portfolios are very common now, but teachers should consider what medium may be the best way to highlight the relevant work pieces.

On my left ankle, I have a tattoo, the Chinese symbol for water. Years ago, I attended an art show and saw a photographic piece called "Be Like Water." When asked why the piece was given that name, the artist said, "Every time I am met with a challenge, my friend tells me to 'Be like water.' In other words, go with the flow." It resonated with me, thus the tattoo.

What does this have to do with anything? When I thought about how to best serve students when it comes to assessment, the idea of choice came to my mind. Students are diverse in their learning needs and thus, assessment should address these needs. What happens to students when given the opportunity to choose how they are assessed? Flow theory happens!

## FLOW THEORY

What *is* flow theory? Flow theory is a concept first coined by psychologist Mihaly Csikszentmihalyi, who noticed how immersed artists became with their work. He also noted how others—such as scientists, athletes, and authors—became so hyper-focused and completely engaged in their work, and he coined this hyper-focus as an "optimal experience" (Csikszentmihalyi, 1990). This notion was studied even further by John Spencer, who shared ways in which flow theory increased student engagement. According to Spencer, flow theory can be used to boost student engagement in the following ways:

- Starting with intrinsic motivation
- Minimizing distractions
- Embracing student choice and agency
- Providing scaffolding
- Helping students monitor progress (Spencer, 2017)

How does this relate to student choice with assessment? When you give students voice and choice with assessment, you are giving students power and control over how they are assessed. Further, students are motivated and immerse themselves in the learning because they want to be able to showcase their skills using an evaluative tool of their choice. They are intrinsically motivated to achieve. Students will showcase their talents if given the opportunity to do so. Our learners will be so immersed in the learning and showcasing their talents that, according to Spencer and Csikszentmihalyi, the students will experience flow, becoming so involved in the assessment activity or project that nothing else will matter and the experience will be fun and enjoyable (Csikszentmihalyi, 1990; Spencer, 2017).

> *"Don't be discouraged by a test score. It takes some students months or even years to grasp particular concepts and realize their full potential. Remember that sometimes our role is to be seed-planters, and that it is more important for you to always believe in your students' full potential, even when others don't."*
>
> —Jody, former ML/EL teacher, Florida

## DESIGNING AN ASSESSMENT SURVEY

All educators have learners with diverse needs and backgrounds. The question is, how can you continue to give them one-size-fits-all assessments when we know they all have different learning needs? Educators differentiate instruction; thus, they must differentiate assessment. How can you begin to do this important work? Following are some starting ideas for consideration:

1. Conduct a survey. I give students a Google Form survey asking them to identify the following:
   a. Strengths
   b. Weaknesses
   c. Talents they may have (drawing, writing, singing, etc.)
2. Ask students their feelings about the following tasks:
   d. Creating a podcast (you might have to explain what a podcast is or provide an example)
   e. Designing comic strips/graphic novels
   f. Creating Flipgrid video recordings (you might have to explain what a Flipgrid is or provide an example)
   g. Engaging in artistic representations (paintings, drawings, dramatic renderings)
3. Ask students what assessment looks like to them or how would they like to be assessed. You might have to define or clarify what assessment is.

Once data is collected, it can be used to plan various projects to assess student learning. As the social studies and science teacher, there were many opportunities for implementing projects for the students. Keep in mind, this is what I chose to do with my students; however, during grade-level meetings with my fellow content-area teachers, I would share ideas with them. In addition, by having various choices for students, being able to tailor assessment to meet the needs of students who required accommodations was possible, since students were able to have a choice.

Assessment choices were created for students with their strengths, weaknesses, and talents in mind. For example, when teaching a unit on invasive species in science, students were given the following assessment choices:

1. Your job: Investigate an invasive species that plagues an area.
2. Create a presentation using *one* of the following:
    a. Google Slides (see the Invasive Species Digital Notebook, the last two slides. Add more if necessary).
    b. Essay: Write a detailed research paper on an invasive species of your choice.
    c. Flipgrid discussion: Record an informational video about an invasive species of your choice.

Once students chose which summative project they wanted to complete, they received a research document to collect their data. Students were able to choose which project suited their talents. Further, students assisted with creating a rubric that was student centered. We worked to agree on the language while maintaining the integrity of the goals and objectives of the project. Even though students chose a different summative project, the rubric was uniform, regardless of what project was chosen. Once students had some control over how they were assessed and graded, that is when flow theory took over and students fully immersed themselves in the learning. The projects and the work students did was exceptional, and they were proud to showcase and share their work with peers.

## Conclusion

We will end on a positive note. Recall in Chapter 1, we discussed deficit speech and how it affects teachers and learners, overall. Let's now connect allowing student choice and assessment to move away from deficit thinking. When assessing our learners, we certainly want to inspire success, which has been the theme of this chapter. Spencer (2016) talks about how a deficit mindset can be changed to a developmental mindset. He shares that "a developmental mindset is where you can approach situations as opportunities to affirm what's right, solve potential problems, and ultimately see things as opportunities to do something creative" (Spencer, 2016). Ultimately, offering students opportunities to show their teachers what they have learned in a modality that is comfortable for them is a creative and innovative idea. While it may take some work for educators, the fruits of their labor will be bountiful if it nurtures, develops, and inspires student success and growth.

So go with the flow . . . and watch our learners *grow*!

## DISCUSSION QUESTIONS

- What is assessment, and what does it mean to you?
- How does assessment affect student learning and achievement?
- How can you make assessment engaging and fun while also collecting useful data and analysis of student achievement? ●

# THE ABCs OF SCHOOL

CHAPTER 4

## I&RS, RTI, MTSS, AND SEL

### Frontloaded Vocabulary

**MTSS:** Multi-tiered systems of support: A framework that provides support to all students, using data to target areas in need of improvement.

**RTI:** Response to intervention: An approach within the MTSS framework providing early and targeted academic or behavioral support to students.

**I&RS:** Intervention and referral services: The process by which teachers collaborate and collect information to share with the child study team when referring a student for screening.

**SEL:** Social-emotional learning: Acquiring and nurturing skills that assist with managing emotions, maintaining relations, and being able to make decisions. ●

*"Sometimes students need to know that teachers are people too. When I first started teaching, one of the first assignments I'd give students was five minutes with Mrs. R. Students were given two weeks to complete this task. They could come see me for five minutes with a buddy or alone, but they had to come and have a conversation with me for at least five minutes. They had to tell me about themselves and in return, I'd tell them a little about me; nothing too personal, of course, but just enough to let them see me as a "person" and not just their teacher. Those five minutes made a huge difference in my relationship with my students. I rarely had discipline issues and they knew I was someone they could talk to if they needed."*

—Veronica, high school EL/ML teacher, New Jersey

Take a moment to reread the preceding vignette and ponder the meaning of the moment. This is an example of making a connection with students, and it is important to the classroom environment. Your students will have educational, behavioral, social, and emotional needs, and they have difficulty sharing their vulnerabilities because students don't always have the language or the ability to identify what their needs are. As the teacher, you must create an environment that is inclusive and conducive to learning, but you must also consider the many needs of the students in your midst. It can be a daunting task, not only for the novice teacher but also the veteran teacher. However, this task is not insurmountable. There is a plethora of systems in place designed to serve a multitude of students in various learning environments with numerous learning needs. Gaining an understanding of how they work and their interconnectedness is necessary. Let's dig deeper and learn more about each of these systems and how you, the novice or experienced teacher, can use these tools to assist your young charges and make education more impactful.

## I&RS (Intervention and Referral Services)

I&RS is the first step to addressing general education students' academic and behavior needs in the classroom setting. At the beginning of the school year, you are in the honeymoon phase. Everyone is excited about the beginning of the school year and enjoying the process of getting to know each other. The teacher and students are bonding with each other and soon, the day-to-day routine falls into place. Students begin to relax, and their personalities begin to become apparent. This is when the teacher starts to take notice of any learning issues that a student may have, and this usually occurs in October or November. In some cases, the teacher may have prior knowledge of a student's academic, social, or behavior struggles. I always spoke to other teachers about my students when I had the class list, just to get an idea of who my students were and what challenges, if any, they had. *But* I also made a point to get to know the students in my own way. If the student's teacher from the previous year noticed any issues the student may have had, there should be documentation and information accessible to give some insight into the student's needs. Some of the documentation that you may find useful is any previous I&RS documentation or learning plans, test data, behavior plans, modifications, of other signification information. This prior knowledge may be helpful to the teacher as they assess the student through a new lens and ponder next steps, if they find that the student is experiencing some difficulties. In any case, once the teacher ascertains that a student may require interventions or services, the first step is to meet with the I&RS committee to discuss the student. I&RS stands for intervention and referral services. The I&RS committee may be a building-wide committee or teachers at each grade level and can collaborate to discuss the student's strengths and areas of improvement (asset-based speech!). Once the teachers meet and dialogue about the student and their needs, an intervention plan may be put into place. Several things occur during this process:

1. Any teacher with concerns about a student will refer the student to the I&RS committee. The committee can be composed of a team of teachers, including a special education teacher and academic intervention teacher, in addition to the guidance counselor, school nurse, and administration, to name a few. These meetings can occur a minimum of once a month. However, based on the needs of the student, these meetings can happen once a week. If a team of teachers are spearheading the process, the meetings can occur weekly during team meetings.
2. During the initial meeting, the teacher will discuss areas of concerns with the I&RS committee. The teacher should be specific about the areas of concern and cite specific examples to the committee. In addition, having examples of student work to support or provided evidence of the area of concern is useful. More than one teacher may refer a student to the I&RS committee. Thus, it is important to share the evidence gathered, because different teachers may have evidence of different issues that may require remediation or intervention. All teachers who are presenting a student to the I&RS committee will need to offer insight about the student's academic or behavior needs. Lastly, teachers may share observations of student performance in their individual classrooms and share information that may show that the student's issues are consistent in each learning environment.
3. In conjunction with the committee, an intervention plan will be made. Teachers will choose two to three interventions to use and monitor the student's progress. If more than one teacher is going through the I&RS process, each teacher will have to choose their own interventions. They may be similar, or they may be different depending on the subject area and the student's needs in that subject area. Teachers can collaborate and discuss the interventions that they are choosing to implement. Each teacher must monitor the use of the interventions put in place to determine whether they are effective. Usually, the interventions are monitored for six to eight weeks, with the teachers incorporating the interventions into their instructions. If there is an academic intervention teacher working with the classroom teacher, they will also incorporate the intervention into instruction.

At the conclusion of the intervention plan, the interventions that were used will be analyzed to ascertain whether the intervention was successful. Teachers should have student work and other evidence to support the usefulness or success of the intervention used during instruction. *But* if the intervention didn't work, the teacher(s) should also have evidence to support that as well. The intervention process is multi-faceted. Let's discuss in more detail what this process looks like.

## RTI (RESPONSE TO INTERVENTION)

> *"I just want to teach the students, and I want to be able to adjust to meet their needs, give them the help they deserve."*
>
> —Joan, sixth-grade ELA teacher, New Jersey

RTI is a framework used to provide students with assistance when struggling academically, socially, emotionally, or otherwise. Teachers use data gleaned from various assessments as well as classroom observation or prior intervention data to identify students in need and prescribe interventions to the students. The framework has three tiers (see Figure 4.1).

**Figure 4.1**

**RTI Pyramid**

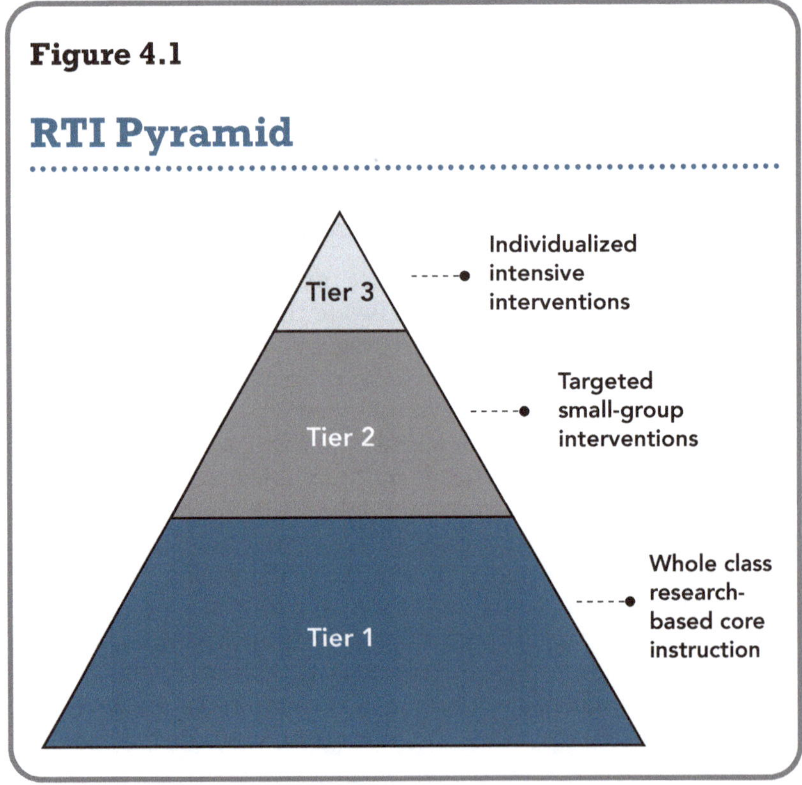

### Tier 1

Students who are on Tier 1 are general education students receiving assistance in the classroom from the general education teacher. These students usually exhibit success when receiving interventions implemented by the teacher over a period, usually six to eight weeks. Teachers select the interventions based on student needs and put a plan into place to implement them. The interventions are tracked and monitored for effectiveness by the teacher and discussed with the I&RS team, especially if more than one teacher is implementing interventions with the same student. If the interventions do not work or are deemed ineffective, another set of interventions is selected and implemented by the teacher. Again, other teachers may also be using interventions in the classroom. If the interventions are not working or continue to be ineffective, students then progress to Tier 2. Please note, that a student can progress to Tier 2 in one subject but may not progress to Tier 2 in another subject if interventions are deemed successful by a teacher in another content area.

### Tier 2

These students continue to receive assistance from the classroom teacher. However, in addition to the interventions put in place by the classroom teacher, an academic intervention or basic skills teacher will provide additional support in the classroom environment. Both teachers review the lesson plans weekly and plan ways to implement and incorporate the interventions into instruction. For the implementation of the interventions to be effective, common planning is necessary. The academic intervention teacher will contribute to the discussion during meetings with the I&RS team to gauge the effectiveness of interventions, and they may also suggest other interventions to implement during instruction. Having the academic intervention teacher assist with the implementation of the intervention strategies is helpful because the student receives concentrated instruction. Further, having another educator involved with implementing the interventions provides information about the student via an alternative lens. If Tier 2 inventions fail to assist the student, the student progresses to the next tier.

### Tier 3

Students who are on Tier 3 require extensive and intensive assistance with interventions. They not only receive assistance in the classroom setting, but they are also pulled by the academic intervention teacher to receive small-group and/or individualized instruction. Interventions that were selected by the classroom teacher and academic intervention teacher are utilized during small-group instruction and tracked. The academic intervention teacher may meet with a minimum of one student and a maximum of three students, for a span of 20 minutes, several times a week, reviewing classroom instruction and providing additional support. Concentrated instruction with the academic intervention teacher is an extension of what transpires in the classroom environment, and students can return to the classroom with skills necessary to participate in the academic setting with their peers.

To gain an understanding of what types of interventions a teacher may use, please see the chart with suggested interventions (see Table 4.1). There are a plethora of activities that may be employed while working with students using the RTI model.

**Table 4.1**

## Intervention Examples

| TIERS | INTERVENTION EXAMPLES |
|---|---|
| Tier 1 | Differentiation of instruction, using graphic organizers, front-loading vocabulary words, giving students breaks, behavior contracts, use of tech tools, to name a few |
| Tier 2 | In addition to those mentioned for Tier 1, guided reading groups, use of flashcards, peer learning groups, mini workshops |
| Tier 3 | In addition to those mentioned for Tiers 1 and 2, weekly check-ins, home/school collaboration with parent/guardian, providing student with a peer mentor |

### *Post-Intervention Evaluation*

If a student is receiving Tier 1, 2, or 3 intervention assistance, at the end of the six- to eight-week cycle, the I&RS committee will reconvene to discuss the interventions used and if they were successful. If they are useful and student progress increases, the teacher may choose to continue with the protocols that were put into place. If the interventions are not useful, the teacher, in conjunction the academic intervention teachers and the I&RS team, can choose new interventions that may aid the student. However, in some cases, the interventions put in place may not work, even after attempting to implement several strategies to assist the student. If the teacher has made several attempts to assist the student and no improvement is made, the next step is to refer the student to the CST (child study team) for analysis and possible screening. Parents are contacted and invited to meet with the I&RS committee and the classroom teacher to discuss options for the student.

Constant communication is necessary so that the parents never feel as though they were not involved in their child's academic process.

## MTSS (MULTI-TIERED SYSTEMS OF SUPPORT)

MTSS is a framework that is an extension of RTI (response to intervention.) While RTI focuses on academics, MTSS is used to provide students with assistance when struggling academically, behaviorally, emotionally, and socially. We have discussed students being referred to the I&RS team for academics. However, students can be referred to the I&RS team for behavioral, emotional, and social matters as well. Teachers can put interventions into place that can assist students in these areas.

With MTSS, several individuals are involved with helping the student to achieve success. Some examples of interventions may include the following:

- The student meets with the guidance counselor on a weekly basis if the student is having social or emotional difficulties. This could include individual or group counseling sessions.
- Provide a student with a timer to assist with finishing assignments, if the student is off task or easily distracted during instruction.
- If a student has several absences or tardies, an intervention would be to create and implement an attendance action plan, with the student and parents.

### *Post-Intervention Evaluation*

Different interventions run the gamut, but the interventions are based on the student's needs. As with RTI, whatever interventions are used must be charted and monitored by the teacher and the I&RS committee. Successful interventions as well as those that are not deemed successful should be tracked so this information can be shared with future classroom teachers. Furthermore, these interventions may lead to involving other parties to ensure the students safety and well-being. For example, if a student needs outside counseling or screening, the information gleaned from the interventions that were put into place could prove useful when trying to assist the student.

## CST (CHILD STUDY TEAM)

Every school has a child study team. The CST is the last part of the intervention process on behalf of the student. CST is comprised of a school social worker, school psychologist, and learning disabilities teacher consultant (LDTC). After the teacher, in conjunction with the I&RS team and other teachers who are working with struggling students, has exhausted all interventions or noted their ineffectiveness, the student will be referred to the CST for evaluation. CST members will review the data and decide if a student should be screened for potential learning disabilities. CST members may also visit the classroom environment to observe students and offer suggestions to the classroom teacher before deciding if the student should be screened or evaluated. There are certain instances when a student may not be screened. For example, students who are multilingual learners or MLs may not be screened initially. EL students do not receive EL instruction when classified. They will continuc to receive services in the EL program for a period before a decision is made to discontinue EL instruction and then progress to the child study team (CST) for evaluation. In addition, the CST may analyze test data and find that a student does not qualify for screening by the CST. If the student is to be screened by the CST, several parties are involved with the process. Several assessments are given that include an IQ test, assessments by speech and language therapists, evaluation by the learning-disabled teacher consultant, cognitive tests, and several other assessments to gauge whether a student will be classified. After being referred for evaluation, the process must be completed within a certain number of days. Parents or guardians must agree to the assessment.

### *Post-Assessment Evaluation*

If the student is classified, an individual education plan or IEP is written, the CST meets with the parents and teachers, and the plan is put into place for implementation. More on IEPs in Chapter 6. It is worth noting that parents can decline services if they choose to do so. Because of the stigma associated with students being classified and receiving services, sometimes parents opt to not allow their child to receive services because they don't want their child to be labeled. In some cases, parents have been taken to court for educational neglect; however, that is not something that occurs often. But it is important to maintain sound data when working to ensure that all students receive a sound education.

## SEL (SOCIAL-EMOTIONAL LEARNING)

Social-emotional learning is an important part of academic success. But it is also necessary to explain why it is an important component of RTI and MTSS. Many teachers address the SEL needs of students as part of a daily routine. They check in with the students and/or do mindfulness activities with their students, which helps create and develop a nurturing environment. In addition, SEL activities engage students and allow teachers to build relationships with their students. SEL activities are also important to the intervention process because these activities provide teachers with information that assist them with advocating and supporting their students on a daily basis. Students who struggle socially, emotionally, or behaviorally benefit from the implementation of SEL activities. Some activities that can be implemented in the classroom and as intervention strategies are as follows:

- **Mindfulness and meditation activities:** Starting the day with quiet meditation allows the students to relax and settle into their day.
- **Journaling:** Using journals gives students the chance to share their feelings in a non-intrusive way. Give students the option of sharing with you. Some students will do so, but do not make it a requirement. Do let students know that they are supported, thus you are building trust with the students.
- **Daily check-ins:** These can exist in many forms, but one idea is to have a sticky-note wall and ask students to write one word to describe how they are feeling that day (see Figure 4.2). Teachers can provide them with a feelings word list because they may not have language to describe how they are feeling. Students should not be required to write their name on the sticky-note, just their feeling word. Teachers can then choose to have a classroom discussion to review some of the words shared.
- **Stress management activities (stress ball, fidget spinner):** Always keep these items readily accessible in your classroom to provide students with tangible items to help them destress.
- **Peer-to-peer buddy checks:** Students should have the opportunity to chat with friends at the beginning of the day. At times, I found out crucial information from buddy checks. The one rule we did not break was if a student told their buddy something that revealed some kind of risk or harm, their buddy would share with the teacher. In this way, I was able to support students who may have been experiencing something serious or trauma-inducing.
- **Classroom walks:** Students were given the opportunity to visit another classroom to see friends or socialize for a few minutes. This broke the monotony of the day and allowed the students a stretch break.
- **Creating a Zen zone or quiet space for students:** A Zen zone or quiet room for students is always useful and provides students with a safe space when necessary (see Images 4.1 and 4.2).

**Figure 4.2**

## Sticky-Note Wall

I fell happy because yesterday it was one of my friends birthday and get to go to their hose.

I feel tired because i went to sleep kinda late yesterday and i woke up around 7 today

i feel tired because i just wokout

today i am feeling sad because my mom left early for work an

today i feel sad because my mom left erley for work and i do not feel great

Today I'm feeling lousy and a little sad because I'm tired and miss my sister

Today I feel happy because I can learn new thing in my classroom

Today I feel tired because I went some places.

i feel angry because i want to sleep.

I feel dizzy but my head is not spinning

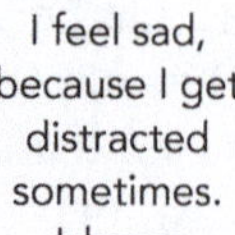


I feel sad, because I get distracted sometimes. Ishawn

I am happy because it is my birthday and I am tried.

Today i feel a little tired

Today I'm feeling tired and kind of sad because I miss my sister.

**Image 4.1**

## Zen Zone 1

**Image 4.2**

## Zen Zone 2

There are a multitude of activities that can be used. Poll the students to gain an understanding of what they enjoy. It is always a good idea to use a tool such as a Google Forms to poll students. With the information gleaned from the poll, you will gain a better understanding of what your students' SEL needs may be. PS: including students in the decision-making process can be considered SEL.

## Conclusion

To conclude, it is important to monitor students in the academic environment so that their needs are better served. With so many diverse learners in your care, this would appear to be a daunting task—and it may be. However, people are in place to assist you as you endeavor to provide interventions and services for those students in need. Tap into the resources and collaborate with your colleagues because you are not alone! There are many other letters of the *school* alphabet that we need to address daily to fully support our students. Look out for the SOS students will send you. It may not always be obvious, but once you receive the call, do your best to assist your students!

## DISCUSSION QUESTIONS

- What are some systems in place that address students' academic and behavior intervention needs?
- How do you engage parents when discussing students' academic and behavioral needs?
- What professional development opportunities would you find beneficial and useful when implementing RTI and MTSS strategies?
- How can technology be used to implement and monitor student progress with RTI and MTSS?
- In addition to student SEL needs, how should educators' SEL needs be addressed? ●

# IMPLEMENTING INCLUSIVE PRACTICES IN THE DIVERSE CLASSROOM

CHAPTER 5

## Frontloaded Vocabulary

**able-bodied:** People who do not have any physical or mental limitations or disabilities.

**access:** The ability to have opportunities regardless of physical, social, economic, and cultural barriers.

**brave spaces:** Brave spaces focus on respect and inclusivity while acknowledging that discomfort and difficult conversations are necessary for growth and learning when dealing with DEAI issues.

**culture:** Shared behaviors, interactions, beliefs and values of a particular group.

**disability:** Any condition that makes it difficult for a person to do certain activities, whether it be physical, intellectual or other.

**diversity:** Human differences that contribute to uniqueness. Diversity includes race, ethnicity, gender, gender identity, sexual orientation, age, social class, physical ability or attributes, and religion, to name a few.

**equality:** Providing what is fair to all.

**equity:** Providing what is necessary to an individual based on their needs.

*(Continued)*

(Continued)

**ethnicity:** A social construct that divides people into smaller social groups based on characteristics, such as values, behavioral patterns, language, political and economic interests, history, and ancestral geographical base.

**gender:** Roles, behaviors, activities, and characteristics that society considers appropriate for men and women.

**identity:** A person's characteristics that makes them recognizable or known.

**inclusion:** Creating environments where any individual or group feels welcomed, respected, supported, and valued and where their differences are embraced and welcomed.

**race:** A social construct that categorizes and characterizes groups of people based on skin color, ancestry, and ethnic affiliation.

**safe spaces:** Relating diversity, equity, and inclusion (DEI), a safe space is an environment where an individual or group feels comfortable expressing themselves without fear of judgment or discrimination or emotional and physical harm.

**sexuality:** Sexual identity, attraction, and behavior. ●

*"I'm a history teacher and I do not claim to be an expert about being an equity educator at all. I'm still learning. In history, it's all about vocabulary. It's not the 'new world' that was 'discovered.' It was a land that was invaded. They aren't 'slaves;' they were enslaved. They didn't 'run away.' They were freedom seekers who self-emancipated. You start with the language you speak, and the language frames the conversation and the history. You change the future by reframing the past."*

—Marcy, educator, Massachusetts

When you first walk into your classroom, you will be charged with the care and education of *all* the students in your midst. It can be overwhelming when you ponder it, but you must think positively. Focus on the potential influence that you will have and how you will impact the lives of your young students. Sitting in front of you will be a diverse population of students. Your young charges will come from all walks of life, with different cultural backgrounds, gifts, abilities, and many other characteristics and traits that will make your classroom a melting pot. This melting pot will prepare students for the future, when they become adult members of society. Learning opportunities in your diverse classroom should be engaging and fun as students get the chance to be exposed to a learning environment that is culturally relevant and inclusive, in preparation for what is to come after they leave your classroom. We'll discuss more on culturally responsive teaching in Chapter 8.

However, as a classroom teacher, designing instruction that addresses the needs of *all* learners can be daunting. Let's ponder Darcy's quote. No one person is an equity expert. No one person will know how to meet the needs of all their students. But one must be *willing* to learn how to address the many needs of your students. It is OK to admit vulnerability, and it is more than OK to ask for help. In doing so, you can find tools and resources that can assist you in creating an inclusive environment for your diverse population of students.

When you look at your students, you visually see them, but you need to truly *see* them. What does that mean? I don't mean "see" your students on the surface. I mean digging deeper and getting to know your students. What are their interests? How can you engage them so that education is impactful? You must consider who and what your students are and what they bring to the classroom daily. Before school begins, take a moment to reflect and consider what a diverse classroom environment entails. One also must understand that diversity is not just about race, culture, and ethnicity. It is about age, gender, ability, physicality, emotions, socioeconomic status, and a plethora of other characteristics and traits. Here are some questions to consider when thinking about the learners you will encounter in your learning environment:

- Who are the students in your classroom?
- Where are they from? What is their cultural and ethnic background?
- What languages do your students speak?
- What cultural celebrations and holidays are important to your students?
- What are their learning styles?
- What talents and gifts do they have?
- What are their learning challenges?
- What is the socioeconomic status of your students?
- What is their gender identity?
- What is their preferred name and/or pronouns?
- If they have a unique name, what does their name mean and how is it significant to their cultural identity?

This is just the tip of the iceberg! There is much to consider when creating a learning environment that is inclusive and welcoming for all learners. In an age where we are witnessing the diminishing of equity and diversity work in curricula and society at large, we must focus on ensuring that we continue this work in the education space so all students are heard and their differences respected and appreciated.

## Leave Your Bias at the Door

A few years ago, a dear friend and colleague who is a fellow edu-warrior, participated in an EdCamp as a presenter at a school district in Central Jersey. He did an activity called A Beliefs Statement Activity, which he adapted from the work of Dr. Edward Fergus, a professor at Rutgers University. Participants answered the belief statements and then the responses were shared anonymously, allowing for deep discussion and self-reflection about personal bias. The experience was illuminating for many and caused participants to think about their own biases as educators.

Everyone experiences some type of bias daily. Long (2016) wrote about a student's experience, where the student went to a testing site and was told that the special education testing room was down the hall. The student didn't identify herself; however, because of the color of her skin, it was assumed that she was a special education student. Society is filled with people who immediately prejudge people based on appearance, age, gender and other traits. Imagine how this must impact the experience of students of color or students who require special services. It harkens back to the activity done by Jane Elliot with her infamous blue eyes and brown eyes experiment. In her book, Elliot (2016) does an experiment where students with a particular eye color are given privileges that their peers with a different eye color will not experience. This experiment highlights the bias that students experience as a result of skin color, ability, or other. When you consider that the teaching population is approximately 79% non-Hispanic white, outnumbering the number of students of color, bias can sometimes creep into the classroom (Schaeffer, 2021). Are there going to be times when you act from a place of bias? Of course. You are human and we are all imperfect. This doesn't make you a "bad" person. The key is to recognize your biases and do something to decrease those instances of bias. How do you make that happen?

### SEEK OUT PROFESSIONAL DEVELOPMENT OPPORTUNITIES

As education professionals, teachers must always reevaluate their practice and find ways to keep learning fun for the students in their midst. Your classroom environment will include students from all walks of life. Many districts have professional development workshops on diversity, equity, and inclusion issues. Participating in these workshops can help any teacher better understand how to identify their biases so that they can create and nurture a healthy environment that is steeped in acceptance. *But* the teacher must be willing to learn and equip themselves with the tools to create an inclusive environment. Students have biases too, so you must take the lead and be the example that they need. Sometimes that means having difficult conversations with others, discussing bias and how to remedy those biases. Sometimes it means recognizing that you must leave your own beliefs at the door because when you walk into the classroom, you are responsible for educating the students and supplying them with a learning environment that is respectful and considerate of all the young people in your midst. That means creating a brave space for students to share without judgment. That means setting parameters for *respectful* discourse. That means *not* treating a student or even a colleague differently because you have dissimilar beliefs and ideologies. You set the tone, and you are the facilitator for creating a nurturing environment for all students you encounter. Impossible? No, it is not, but you must certainly be intentional! See the chart that was shared with participants of a workshop that I facilitated as a guideline to creating an inclusive classroom environment (see Figure 5.1).

**Figure 5.1**

## Creating an Inclusive Classroom Environment

| Dos | Don'ts |
|---|---|
| **DO** activities that address the diversity and various needs of your students in the classroom. | **DON'T** do activities that will make students uncomfortable or single them out. |
| **DO** include students when setting guidelines for an inclusive classroom environment. | **DON'T** insert your personal beliefs into a lesson or conversation. This can be a challenge. |
| **DO** survey students to gain information that will be useful in creating a student-centered environment. | **DON'T** invalidate a student's feelings or emotions. Hear them out and seek guidance if you need assistance. |
| **DO** seek assistance from district DEAI resources and personnel if you have questions or concerns. | **DON'T** be afraid to ask for help. |

In addition, take the reins! As we see the elimination of DEI in many states as well as the eschewing of having conversations about diversity, equity, access, and inclusion, sometimes educators must work together to engage in these discussions. Book clubs are a great way to engage in this work. I worked with a group of teachers to create a book club that was a space for us to engage in necessary dialogue. We created a Google Site to help facilitate the conversation. I also created a Wakelet digital bulletin board when presenting a workshop titled "Social Justice: Using Book Clubs & Other Media to Engage in Discussions About Race" (see Image 5.1).

**Image 5.1**

## Wakelet Bulletin Board

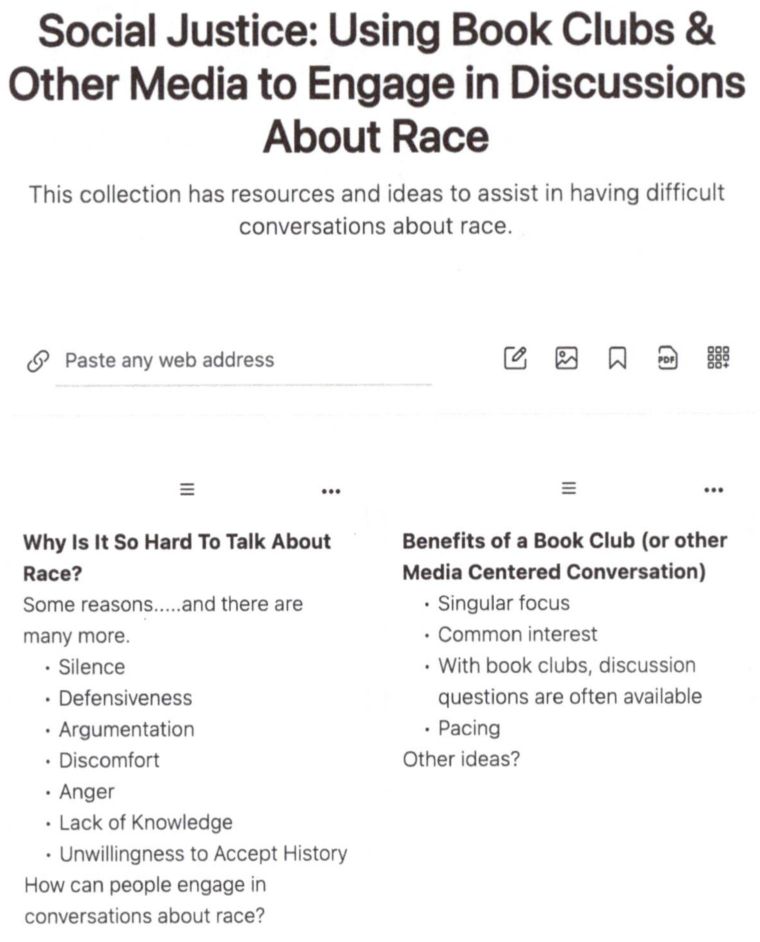

# Social Justice: Using Book Clubs & Other Media to Engage in Discussions About Race

This collection has resources and ideas to assist in having difficult conversations about race.

Paste any web address

**Why Is It So Hard To Talk About Race?**

Some reasons.....and there are many more.

- Silence
- Defensiveness
- Argumentation
- Discomfort
- Anger
- Lack of Knowledge
- Unwillingness to Accept History

How can people engage in conversations about race?

**Benefits of a Book Club (or other Media Centered Conversation)**

- Singular focus
- Common interest
- With book clubs, discussion questions are often available
- Pacing

Other ideas?

## DIVERSE CURRICULA

Students should be exposed to curricula that addresses diversity. Students want to be exposed to curricula that mirrors who they are as individuals. A great resource for teachers is the Global Read Aloud, which was founded by Pernille Ripp. This is an effective way to appreciate diversity because the books chosen address diversity. In addition, the selections speak to different student abilities and learning styles because there are also picture books that address the needs of the visual learner. One year my colleagues and I read the book *A Bridge Home*, by Padma Venkatraman for the Global Read Aloud. The country India was the setting of the book, and the protagonists were female. Students read the book in language arts classes. As the social studies teacher, I used the book to teach two units in the curriculum, Thinking Like a Historian, which taught about research and the use of primary and secondary resources, and Thinking Like a Geographer, which focused on geography skills. For the geography unit, students studied land features and India, identifying land features found in the country. Students also used primary and secondary resources to create a travel brochure highlighting the country of India. In addition, I was also the science teacher, and in science class, students studied the infrastructure of India's water system because we were also studying the Global Goals Initiative and our goal was Goal 14, Life Below Water. Students did projects that addressed the issues with the water system in India. Students created projects that included posters and even podcasts that addressed the water crisis in India. During mathematics class, students discussed what math was like in India and researched mathematicians who were from India. In addition, the music teacher introduced the students to Indian music and songs, and the art teacher had the students create art projects that was akin to Indian art. They also looked at clothing, such as saris, through the lens of artistic expression. Why am I highlighting all these activities? These activities developed and implemented during the Global Read Aloud showcases diversity and how students can be exposed to various cultures and learn about gender roles and other topics relative to diversity in a fun and creative way.

During the unit, the students involved had a great time because they were fully immersed in the study of India and learned a great deal about a different culture. They were able to have discussions and compare and contrast India to their respective cultures. Prior to engaging in this unit, we watched a TED Talk, *Danger of a Single Story*, which is a perfect representation of what bias is. We exposed students to this because we wanted them to learn about India with fresh eyes . . . leaving biases at the door! This is one example of how to learn about another culture and negate bias, because the students *did* have some biases prior to engaging in the learning. But by diversifying curricula, you can afford students the opportunity to have experiences that are all inclusive and chip away at these biases.

Planning and implementing the units took some time. Collaboration was key, and the ELA teacher and I made sure to use common planning time to work together. One of the resources that is easy to use with planning is the tool found on Learning for Justice website. Using the Learning Plan Builder, a lesson can be created based on the four domains of the Social Justice Standards (identity, diversity, justice, and action). In addition, the Learning Plan Builder allows you to access meaningful student texts and choose how you'll teach them and how you'll assess student learning. It is a tool that I have used with graduate students and educators to stimulate ideas and create meaningful learning experiences for our students.

## SUPPORT STUDENT IDENTITIES

This is probably the *most* important thing an educator can do in the classroom. Our students have so many differences, they run the gamut. Identities are based on culture, ability, gender, ethnicity and more. As the teacher, you must accept your students and support them. Using surveys and *getting to know you* activities will help you access information that you can use to assist you with connecting with your students. Simply using a Google form can help you with this goal. You may not have the same beliefs and ideals as the students you teach or their families. Some teachers have had difficulties separating their beliefs from that of the students. It is not our jobs to sway students and indoctrinate them into *our* individual way of thinking. Our responsibility is to educate, support, and nurture differences by creating a nurturing and supportive environment. If your students see this behavior, they will follow your lead. Teachers should not be afraid to use their resources, such as the guidance counselor, school psychologist, or parent liaison, because you won't always have the answers. Your school support system can help and come to your classroom to facilitate conversations with students to assist you with difficult conversations. Be prepared to point students in the right direction if they need support and you can't adequately provide it. That doesn't make you a failure. Providing students with the support they need is one of the best things you can do as an educator (see Table 5.1 and Image 5.2).

**Table 5.1**

### How to Create Identity-Safe Schools and Classrooms

| How to Create Identity-Safe Schools and Classrooms |
|---|
| Promote trust and interpersonal connection: Engage in practices that create trusting relationships and interpersonal connection between educators and students. Find ways to build empathy using connection-building tools. |
| Creating purposeful communities of care and consistency: Identity-safe classrooms and schools cultivate a community of care. Students are seen and valued. By Implementing routines, such as community meetings or creating identity-affirming forums and clubs, a sense of belonging for students, particularly those who identify with minoritized groups, can be established. |
| Creating trusting relationships using restorative practices: Use restorative practice approaches to build trusting and healthy relationships with students. This sense of community can prevent and address conflict and wrongdoing. |
| Promoting understanding, voice, and responsibility: Engage students in demanding inquiries, giving them choice, voice, and growing responsibility for their own learning, which can foster identity safety. |
| Elevating diversity as a resource for learning: Celebrate the unique differences of your students by having culture celebrations and forging connections with students and families. |

Hernández & Darling-Hammond (2022).

**Image 5.2**

## Ruby Bridges Word Wall Sharing Activity With Students

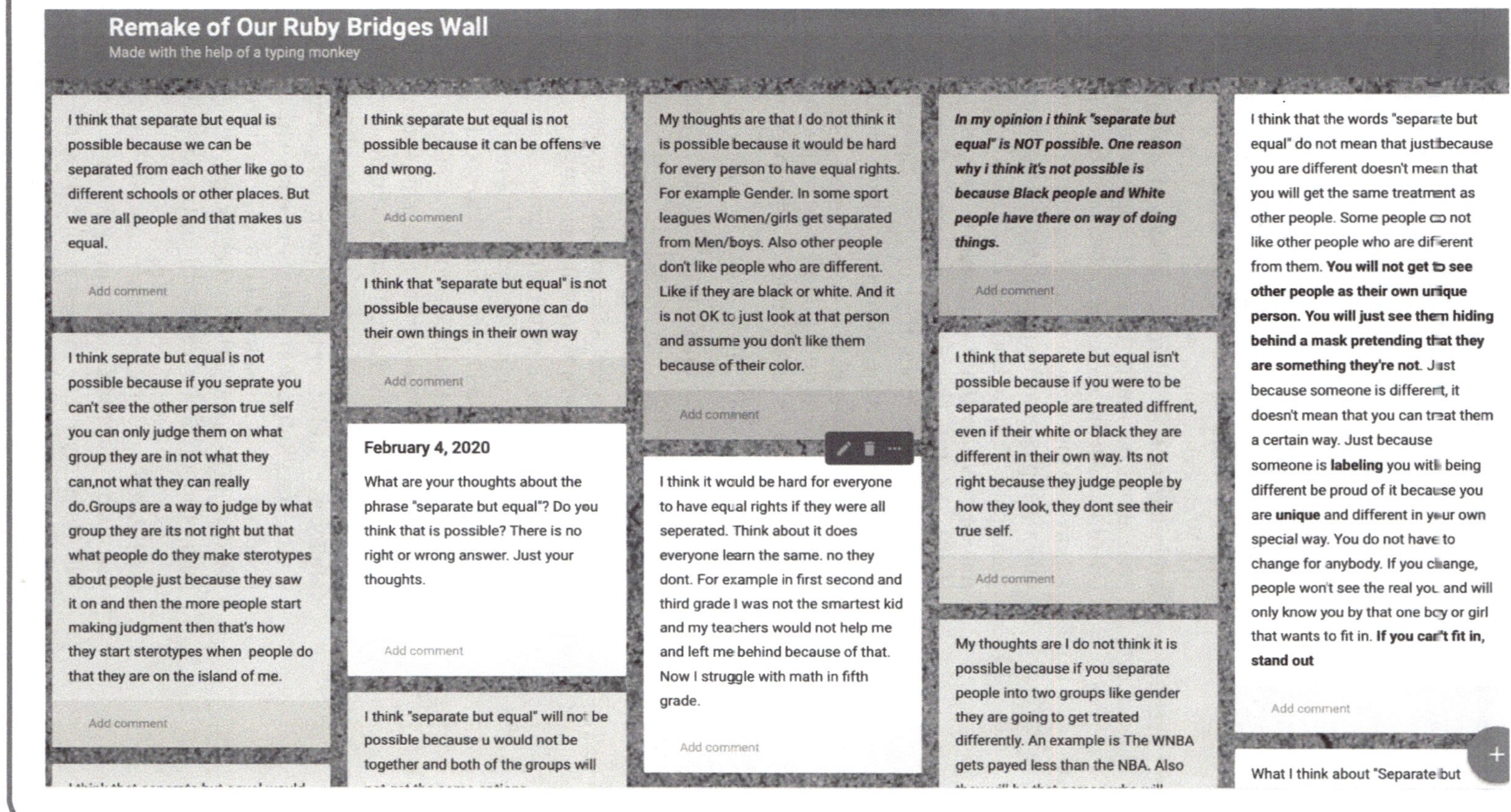

## SAFE SPACES VERSUS BRAVE SPACES

When you think about safe spaces, you probably envision an environment where someone feels they can speak their truth and be protected by those around them. There's this perception that someone will "have your back" or advocate for you when you need assistance. However, when you ponder it, there really is no such thing as a safe space because there will *always* be someone who has a different idea or perception about a topic, especially when we speak about cultural diversity, equity, access, and inclusion. That is OK, because we don't live in a world where everyone agrees. That is completely unrealistic!! With brave spaces, students can truly lay bare their thoughts and emotions, challenging others in a respectful way without concern about backlash. This is the outspoken individuals who feel confident in their process and beliefs and have no issues with sharing In a brave space, everyone can agree to disagree and understand that difficult topics may be broached. In a brave space, students will speak their truth, despite knowing that they may be met with resistance and maybe even hostility. Uncomfortable conversations will be had and that is OK. It is how people engage in these uncomfortable and challenging conversations that matters. Growth and change may come from these thought-provoking topics. Students and teachers may have the capacity to agree to disagree and that is fine. The point is to being confident enough to share your voice and be able to express yourself in any space, without disrespect or disregard for another's thoughts or beliefs.

The idea of a safe space and a brave space intertwine. Creating an environment where students feel safe enough to embrace being brave and challenging the status quo is what you want to do. No topic is safe, *but* students feel safe because they are in a classroom with their peers and teachers who will encourage you to be brave enough to speak up and speak out. Being brave is very difficult because people can and will have differing viewpoints and that is fine. But sometimes, students do not feel brave enough to speak their truth and share their beliefs. That is when the classroom teacher takes the reins and creates the space that allows courage in a safe setting. They go hand in hand. The only way to nurture an environment that is steeped in inclusivity is by having necessary conversations about race, ethnicity, gender, ability, age, and other topics that may be sensitive. As the teacher, you are the facilitator. You assist students with creating an environment conducive to being safe and brave. But remember to leave your bias at the door!! Do *not* insert your beliefs into the conversation but *do* guide your students to be respectful in the classroom environment.

Lastly, to create this environment, it is a good idea to create guidelines and protocols for conversations about difficult topics in the classroom (see Figure 5.2). Students must be mindful of the language they use when in engaging in healthy discourse. Part of giving students voice is allowing them to assist with creating these guidelines. What is accepted and what are the non-negotiables? What language will students use when disagreeing with one another? This is important, and it is a good idea to engage students when making the classroom parameters for having difficult conversations. Furthermore, it is also a good idea to share with parents and guardians when you plan to engage the students in difficult conversations. Some of the conversations to be had are curriculum based because there are standards that address diversity. As the classroom teacher, it is imperative that these standards are met, and parents should be made aware of mandates that require teachers and educators to teach these particular standards.

**Figure 5.2**

### Safe Versus Brave Spaces

| Safe Space Practices Being Able To | Brave Space Practices Being Able To |
|---|---|
| Agree to disagree | Engage in civil discourse |
| Not launch personal attacks at peers | Differentiate between people and concepts |
| Not take things personally | Protect your peace |
| Be respectful of others | Be responsible for your intentions |
| Assume the positive intentions of others | Be responsible for your potential impact |
| Being in a "safe space" means sharing your thoughts and ideas but being comfortable and not pushing the envelope. Being in a brave space means sharing your thoughts and ideas, pushing the envelope, and engaging in discomfort but in a respectful way that may inspire growth. | |

## Conclusion

In conclusion, it can be difficult to have conversations about diversity, equity, access, and inclusion. We are currently seeing the elimination of DEI in some companies and in the realm of education. However, it is important to address the needs of the students in our midst, because our classrooms are diverse. They are filled with students who have various needs and abilities and who come from varied backgrounds. Students want to be recognized and respected. Students deserve to see themselves reflected in all aspects of the school environment and the curricula. As educators, it is our responsibility to encourage an environment for all, because that is truly what education is all about: Learning for all, by all.

## DISCUSSION QUESTIONS

- How do *you* define diversity?
- What are the characteristics of a classroom that addresses the needs of your diverse student population?
- Consider any biases that you may have regarding the students in your classroom. How do you address those biases? ●

CHAPTER 6

# ACCESS AND INCLUSION FOR LEARNERS WITH DIVERSE NEEDS

## Frontloaded Vocabulary

**scaffolds:** These are types of supports provided for learners to help them access learning. These may be academic, language, social, or behavioral ways that assist learners as they work with concepts or skills that may be just beyond what they can independently do. It is important to note that scaffolds should only be the least amount of support that any learner needs—for only as long as they need it.

**self-efficacy:** These are feelings that one can be successful in a particular situation.

**differentiation of instruction:** This term refers to providing different types of teaching and learning experiences for learners based on their strengths and needs. Ideally, all learners are working toward the same objectives or goals but have different pathways and supports in achieving them. ●

As discussed in Chapter 5, when we say *diverse*, this viewpoint is often from a very Eurocentric perspective. From this perception, diversity may include anyone or anything that is different from the perceived "norm" or the majority population. According to Howe and Lisi (2023), eurocentrism highlights the experience dominated by "Anglo, male, middle class, and Protestant thinking" people (p. 16). Diversity is also usually connected with languages or cultures that may be different from the majority community. However, if we step back and consider objectively the differences in our school communities, we see that every student is diverse or unique in some way. (*"Who am I to say that someone else's perspective or individuality is diverse? Why would my perception be considered to be the norm or what is mainstream?"*)

A learner's diverse perspectives may include (but are not limited to) academic differences, languages, culture, race, ethnicities, medical/physical differences, educational experiences, family dynamics, interests, talents, and preferences, and the list can go on. Since we begin with the premise that the educators must acknowledge that their perspective should not be considered the starting point, every learner in all schools must be viewed as unique and diverse.

How we refer to these learners is of supreme importance and goes beyond a category. Educators should strive for "person-first" language, as you will see in this chapter, rather than description-first language. Table 6.1 shows the difference.

**Table 6.1**

## Differences of Descriptions/ Perceptions and Person-First language

| DESCRIPTION-FIRST LANGUAGE | PERSON-FIRST LANGUAGE |
|---|---|
| Poor person | Person with a low income; person whose income falls below the federal poverty threshold |
| Homeless person | Person who is unhoused; person who is experiencing homelessness |
| High-school dropout | Person with less than a high school education |
| Handicapped person | Person with a disability or specific challenge |

Many people feel that this emphasizes a person's humanity over their disability. However, within various communities, people have their own preferences of how they are described. Some people in the autism community prefer to be called an "autistic person" instead, as they may consider autism to be a defining characteristic of theirs. There are also many variations of preferences in expressing that a person has a hearing impairment. Asking a person (age relevantly) and respecting their wishes is paramount to any training or preferences we feel. This is one of those times that we set aside our own preferences and *listen!*

## Ten Commandments of Inclusion

As inclusion is often a misunderstood concept, the following is a list of guidelines to aid in reflection and true conversation regarding the benefits of inclusion for many learners (Furlong, 2022a).

### #1: ALL LEARNERS HAVE THE RIGHT TO THE EDUCATION THAT IS MOST APPROPRIATE TO THEIR NEEDS.

There are times in which the learners' needs are viewed through the lens of what is available or convenient for schools. Individualized Education Plans (IEPs) must truly represent the unique needs of the learner—not a representation of the programs that are offered already or a school schedule that is already made. All learners—with IEPs or not—are entitled to instruction that helps them grow and learn. As defined by the United States Department of Education Office for Civil Rights, this free appropriate public education (FAPE) goes much beyond the classroom structure, and equity for all learners should be considered in every decision made in the school community. As we consider inclusion in the broadest sense, we must find ways to make sure all learners have access to appropriate education that provides them with an inclusive school experience—both in the classroom and out.

### #2: ALL LEARNERS HAVE THE RIGHT TO HIGHLY QUALIFIED CONTENT-AREA TEACHERS OR SPECIALISTS WHO ARE TRAINED IN INCLUSION AND COTEACHING.

There are two assertions in this statement: that all teachers must teach in areas where they are experts and that explicit training in coteaching is necessary. First, not only must teachers have the content-area knowledge they need to adequately teach their learners, but they also must have the support in learning how to best work with colleagues to make content and language accessible for all learners. This type of training must be part of annual professional learning to ensure all collaborative teaching pairs/groups have the opportunity to establish guidelines particular to their learners that year.

## #3: ACCESS TO GRADE-LEVEL CURRICULA FOR EVERYONE IS CRUCIAL FOR EVERY LEARNER.

Sometimes some learners need reinforcement in concepts or skills typically associated with previous grades. It is necessary to teach learners what they need to learn, especially when considering foundational skills. With that being said, all learners are entitled to access to grade-level curriculum and standards—although these interactions with content may look different for learners with different strengths. It is the responsibility of the educators to ensure that they receive the scaffolds/supports necessary to have those interactions with the same curricula as their peers of the same age. This is necessary both to ensure that learning is age-relevant and that appropriate concepts are learned as foundational knowledge for future instruction.

## #4: ALL LEARNERS BELONG. ALL TEACHERS BELONG.

The classroom (or school!) doesn't "belong" to the general education learners, and the learners with diverse needs are not visitors in this space—no matter the amount of time that any student spends in the physical space. When groups of people (teachers and learners in this example) feel ownership over a physical space, the balance of power is skewed. No group should feel that they are more entitled to belonging and have more ownership than anyone else. If there are learners who are coming and going from the classroom space, it is to get the support that meets their unique needs in the classroom and beyond. These learners must feel support and belonging in all their learning environments.

## #5: THE OBJECTIVES ARE THE SAME FOR ALL LEARNERS; THE WAY DIFFERENT LEARNERS ACHIEVE THE OBJECTIVES MAY VARY.

As noted previously, all learners must have experiences and instruction with grade-relevant content. The objectives of all lessons are guidelines linked to district curricula and state standards. However, there is flexibility in how learners access this grade-level content, and this is where attention to the diverse needs of all learners is considered. There are many ways that learners can engage with the same topic in different ways. Considering the strengths, interests, and individual needs of one's learners should drive all activities and assessments.

## #6: ALL TEACHERS ARE RESPONSIBLE FOR ALL LEARNERS IN THE CLASS.

Historically, there has sometimes been a delineation or separation between "my students" and the students that belong to the *other* teachers. (*"Those students aren't my responsibility." "I don't know those students in my class; they belong to my coteacher."*) When one considers inclusion, this must not be the accepted culture in any classroom or school; this leads to the toxic environment in which some learners feel more of a connection to the school community than others. While there are times in which some teachers have particular sets of learners on their rosters or in their gradebook—particularly when considering learners with IEPs or specific accommodations—there should never be a time in which all educators do not take responsibility for the well-being and learning of all learners.

## #7: COTEACHERS MUST HAVE TIME TOGETHER WITHIN THEIR CONTRACTUAL DAY IN WHICH THEY CAN PLAN.

While this may be an extremely idealistic guideline for inclusion due to scheduling and other challenges, it is critical to the success of the coteaching team that they have dedicated time to plan and prepare together. This type of collaboration is necessary to keep the balance of power (and workload) from influencing the coteaching relationship in a negative way. This type of acknowledgement in the creation of schedules is just one way that a district demonstrates that inclusion and coteaching are valued and important.

## #8: NO LEARNERS ARE MARGINALIZED (GEOGRAPHICALLY, ACADEMICALLY, OR SOCIALLY) IN THE CLASS.

One may think that clustering learners with similar needs in a specific section of the classroom (back corner, anyone?) may be an efficient way to provide targeted support. However, when learners with different needs are seated together in a classroom in a particular area, they are removed from their peers in a way that is marginalizing—geographically, academically, and socially. These learners should be strategically seated amongst their general education peers to facilitate interaction, connections, and friendships among them. Also, when all learners are "interspersed" among their peers in a classroom, it is more likely that educators will engage them in relevant discussions and activities alongside one another. When planning activities for class that are meant to engage learners in fun ways to learn, access for everyone must be a priority.

## #9: DIVERSITY IS VALUED AND CELEBRATED IN CLASS AND IN THE SCHOOL COMMUNITY.

It would be rare to find someone who says they do not value diversity. However, many of those same people may have difficulty articulating what celebrating diversity may look like in educational settings beyond acknowledging specific months. First and foremost, all learners must be able to see themselves as members of a community in which they *belong*. It is up to the educators to foster the environment that supports that. This can be done in a few ways:

1. **Exploring literature and curricula that represent the learners in the class/school and other groups.** It is wonderful to have experiences in which our learners (and teachers!) can engage with learning about other perspectives represented in the world, but it is crucial that the diversity of the community is directly related to what they read and experience.
2. **Having physical environments that not only teach about diversity but are interwoven in the thread of the community.** Signs should be in different languages. Student projects should be displayed. Art and music should build connections among communities. Locations of different learning environments should not be isolated from general education classrooms. All areas of the school must be accessible to people of different abilities.
3. **Ensuring social-emotional learning (SEL) is authentic, accessible, and inclusive to all learners.** This may mean lessons are available in different formats or languages and must support **SEMH** (social-emotional mental health) of all learners.

## #10: ADMINISTRATION MUST BE KNOWLEDGEABLE AND STRONG PROPONENTS OF COTEACHING MODELS.

A supportive environment that firmly advocates for professional collaboration must be driven by the administration. Not only do administrators need to be knowledgeable about coteaching so they can effectively provide support to teachers, but this is crucial as they do observations and evaluations of them while teaching in these situations. Kampen (2022) describes the following options in terms of coteaching with two or more educators in the classroom at a given time.

- Parallel teaching: The class is split into small groups, each with an educator who is simultaneously teaching the same lesson at the same time to their respective groups. This model may allow teachers to better answer questions and tailor their instruction to the needs of their smaller set of students.
- Station teaching: Within this model, there are at least two different stations in the classroom in which students either work independently or with one of the teachers in the room on different activities. Most often, these stations are varying experiences with regards to the same topic or similar skills. Students rotate to ensure all learners have the opportunity for support or independent practice in the same way. Independent practice may include writing or listening to audiobooks, if that is relevant to the content.
- Team teaching: Teachers are both at the front of the room and maneuvering within the classroom in this model. There isn't a "main" or lead teacher in this scenario, and all teachers are supporting all students. In terms of presenting content, teachers take turns and support one another while teaching.
- Alternative teaching: Class is split into two or more groups (depending on the number of educators in the room) with one group being larger than the others. The large group engages in general instruction with the smaller groups participating in smaller, more targeted instruction to meet individual needs.
- One teaches, one observes: This may be the least common of the coteaching models, but this may be what you experience as a new teacher if a coach comes to support you. One teacher is at the center of instruction and another teacher is observing and taking notes/data meant to drive future instruction. This second teacher is moving amongst the students and noting what students may need.
- One teaches, one assists: This method is like the one above but the second (or third) teacher in the room is engaging with students and assisting as needed. They may also be taking notes and data, but their primary responsibility is providing access to the lesson for all learners.

It is important that all stakeholders in the school understand the coteaching models and the ways that educators shift instruction to meet the needs of all learners. It is not uncommon that many of these models are utilized in one day (or one lesson!), based on the varying activities and students' needs.

As administrators and policymakers create schedules, select educational programs, and make decisions that affect the entire school culture, they are key in the implementation of educational models that fit the diverse needs of learners. We cannot fit the learners' needs into an already existing model; it will for sure sacrifice what may be best for some learners of any given year. Admin must also be willing to attend training with teachers to best understand coteaching, inclusion, and the flexibility that comes with a dynamic model of adjusting to what is best for learners.

*"I have made my personal improvement plan for this year to really engage with coteaching teams in new ways. I am learning about the different dynamics of the content-area teachers and the specialists who teach alongside them. In the past, there have been issues with communication, and I want to be on the team to support this very important shift."*

—Susanna, academic coach, Pennsylvania

## Academic Diversity Designations

There are some designations at the district or school level that may give some more specific information about our learners. Sometimes these labels may guide class placement or determine the types of services or supports that learners need. Hallahan et al. (2020) refer to learners with needs outside the norm as exceptional learners, and we maintain that this includes those with learning differences, language diversity, and those who may qualify for gifted and talented programs. If these labels are not considered to be a lifelong "sentence," they can be viewed simply as providing background about how educators can best design their instruction. It is crucial that all stakeholders understand that these designations must not come with preconceived notions or with stigmas attached; in fact, this mindset must inform every decision they make. In this section, we will cover the most common designation terms.

*"As a middle-school teacher, I know that kids' personalities are emerging, and they may be less 'loveable' at certain times. In the beginning of one year, I had one student who I just couldn't tell if he was a bit disrespectful or was just very forthcoming and up front with his opinions. I spoke*

*with my in-class support teacher, and she shared with me that he is on the autism spectrum. While this did not change my expectations for academics or behavior for him, this gave a bit of context to his social interactions. With this information, I saw a bigger picture of this child and we had a great year together. When people say that we should never discuss labels for students, I always think of this student and how this was a way of communicating ways I could support him."*

—Joseph, educator, New York

## Learners With IEPs

These learners are those who qualify for special education services for any one of a variety of reasons. Programs for these learners are federally regulated through laws, such as IDEA (Individuals with Disabilities Education Act). When a learner is determined to be eligible for these programs or services, a team of experts (including their parents) convenes to construct a document called an Individualized Education Plan (IEP). Learners over 14 are also encouraged to be an active vocal part of this team. This document is drafted following evaluations that determine eligibility for services, and it includes specific information about the evaluation results, goals, and accommodations to which this learner is entitled. There is also feedback from teachers and other related service professionals that is both anecdotal (stories and observations) and data driven.

Typically, this IEP team meets annually, and evaluations are performed every three years. The plan and evaluations may change based on the growth and needs of the learner. This document is considered a living document, meaning it may be updated or changed at any time. As the parents are crucial members of this team, it is important that they have access to all evaluations and are invited to all meetings. If the parents' language is different from the one used in the meetings, certified translation services must be provided.

When speaking about eligibility for special education services, it is almost inevitable that law and specific guidelines are brought into the conversation. Placements for learners with IEPs are to represent the LRE (least restrictive environment). This refers to the variety or types of classrooms and learning spaces to which learners with IEPs may have access. The following (Figure 6.1) are some of the options from least to more restrictive.

**Figure 6.1**

## Least Restrictive Environment

| |
|---|
| This placement provides for the learner to be in the presence of general education peers for more than 80% of the school day. A special education teacher joins the general education teacher in the classroom for either the full day or for certain classes. Paraprofessionals often also provide support within this model. Learners work on grade-level skills/concepts with appropriate accommodations and modifications to bridge any difficulties in accessing the material. |
| Learners who need more intense support than what they could typically receive in a general education classroom may leave that setting for specific classes. For these classes, they learn in a small group taught by a special education teacher. |
| This type of placement would be necessary for learners whose academic, behavioral, social, or medical needs exceed what they could receive in either a general education class or a resource room. Learners typically receive all their instruction in the same classroom and leave for related services. Ideally, schedules align with grade-level peers to attend classes like art, gym, and music, possibly wih an aide from their class attending to support them. |
| The learner is placed in a program either in another district or in a school that is designed for learners who need similar supports. With consideration of LRE, often this placement is considered only after other options have not been successful. |

There are some learners who would thrive in an inclusion setting while others would benefit from more structured supports. The LRE considers the learner's specific needs and does not make assumptions based on their diagnosis or other factors. Reflections on a learner's placement should be happening constantly with the learner's best interests in mind. This may be where—as you gain confidence and knowledge—you become the advocate for your learners and their families.

## Learners With 504 Plans

A 504 plan supports a learner with a medical diagnosis that affects their educational experiences. These experiences may be specific to academics, or they may extend beyond classroom learning.

Typically, a learner does not have both an IEP and a 504 plan (as they cover some of the same things), but there are exceptions. A 504 plan may be designed with the school guidance counselor or another representative of the general education support team, while an IEP is created through the child study team with special education educators.

> *"When my son had a series of medical events (some of which happened in school), the guidance counselor helped me set up a 504 plan for him. This plan allowed him to advocate for himself and his health needs without feeling as if he was asking for special treatment or a favor. First and foremost, this plan was a means of communication between our family and the educators on his team."*
>
> —Denise

The following (Table 6.2) are some examples of medical issues that may necessitate a 504 plan. Of course, every child's needs are unique, and most 504 plans have more than one or two accommodations.

**Table 6.2**

## Sample 504 Plans and Sample Accommodations

| MEDICAL DIAGNOSES | ACCOMMODATION(S) |
|---|---|
| ADHD (Attention-Deficit/Hyperactivity Disorder) | • Extended time on tests or frequent breaks<br>• They may also have fidget devices at their desk or permission to work standing up |
| Diabetes | • Permission to have food or drink at their desk<br>• Unlimited restroom breaks<br>• Regular trips to the nurse |
| Seizures | • Shorter assignments<br>• Exemption from standing in front of the room for presentations to prevent episodes or exhaustion |
| Any form of physical disability | • Specific plans in case of an emergency (evacuation/fire drill)<br>• Modifications or exemptions for engaging in any kind of physical education |

*"Unfortunately, while my son was in day care, even though it was a nut-free facility, we had numerous 'incidents' with his allergies since he has other food allergies as well. I was nervous for him to begin elementary school, which was not nut-free. As I explained some of my concerns to the school nurse—that he has a wheat allergy so he can't use Play-Doh or make pasta art, he wouldn't be able to do science experiments or math with beans because of a legume allergy, in addition to his nut and peanut allergies—she suggested we create a 504 plan for him. This would make sure that everyone in the school would be informed of all his allergies. I was able to add in some other accommodations that were a concern of mine, such as being [a] chaperone on field trips, so I could monitor a new environment for allergens. The nurse, school counselor, classroom teacher, principal, and myself were all part of the team that wrote the 504. It was a great relief to have that document and be included in writing his plan. We revisit it every year and have made adjustments for allergies he's outgrown and new classes he'll be taking as he gets older. I am really grateful for the input of each member of the team, and truly believe that this has helped to avoid incidents at this school."*

—Sarah, bilingual educator and parent, New Jersey

Consider the 504 plan as the guidebook of what a learner needs to be safe and successful in your classroom and school. Like an IEP, these documents are living documents that may be updated at any time, so if anyone on this team thinks of something that would be beneficial to this learner, it may be added at any point in the year. It is particularly important to consider at the beginning of each school year the increased responsibilities or different expectations that may be present.

## Learners Who Are Eligible for Enrichment Programs

Often when we talk about learners with diverse needs, we don't mention learners whose needs include designing appropriate instruction that would provide the right level of challenge for them. Many districts use multiple measures that include standardized testing to determine eligibility for enrichment programs. These learners may be considered "gifted" in all areas or in certain subjects.

Some *gifted and talented* programs require learners to be placed together in the same class(es) throughout the day, and the enrichment instruction is provided for all learners. Other programs have these learners placed into various classes but pulled out for small-group enrichment or to receive it through differentiated instruction in the classroom. As learners move to older grades where they may be taking different math courses (algebra, rather than basic math, for example), the former model may be more common.

It is important to acknowledge that the needs of these learners are the same as the needs of all learners: They must be challenged appropriately, have opportunities to collaborate with their peers, engage in high-interest experiences that provide them with opportunities to analyze and create, and feel empowered in their learning. Within these we find ways to meet these very different needs of our learners.

Considering that these learners have needs that are just as unique as their peers, we must look at the whole child when designing instruction that is appropriate for them. Some are gifted in all areas of the curriculum and others have strengths where they should be challenged and difficulties in other areas.

## Multilingual Learners

English learners (now often referred to as *multilingual learners [ML] or emergent bilinguals*) represent an extremely diverse group of learners. These learners may come from different countries, educational backgrounds, and cultures. They may have different levels of English proficiency or backgrounds in literacy in any language. Important to note is that even the learners who may speak the same language or come from the same part of the world may have very different strengths and challenges. More in-depth discussion about multilingual learners can be found in Chapter 7.

When considering inclusion for multilingual learners, many more schools are providing support in the general education classroom to increase opportunities to engage in grade-relevant work alongside their peers. While some support may leverage learners' heritage languages, other ways to provide access would be sheltered English strategies. With these techniques, learners are acquiring the language and content of the class with explicit instruction for each.

Programs that allow for flexibility to meet the unique needs of multilingual learners are often the most successful. While it is ideal to ensure the most exposure possible to grade-level peers, there are situations in which MLs may benefit from small-group or individualized instruction outside the general education classroom for short periods of time. As we say with all models of instruction, educators must always have the best interests of the learners at the forefront of everything we do. We will dive deeper into the specific needs of English learners and multilingual learners in Chapter 7.

*"As over and underrepresentation in special education programming remains an issue for the multilingual learner community, it can be intimidating and overwhelming for English as a second language educators to navigate the identification process and understand the intersection of SPED and ESL. Multilingual learners are an asset in our classrooms, with their rich cultural and linguistic histories and experiences, but the systems of RTI and the special education identification process were not necessarily designed with these diverse learners and their unique needs in mind. Crafting IEPs that address the cultural and linguistic needs of these learners is necessary for their educational success, and therefore a practice that needs to become the norm in our school systems."*

—Gillian, EL/ML educator, New Jersey

## General Education Learners

General education learners typically include learners who do not fit the criteria for eligibility for exceptional (outside the "norm") programs such as the ones previously described. This, however, does not mean that they may not have a variety of needs or strengths; the nature of education is to celebrate the uniqueness of all learners.

Rather than imagining that the general education learners would represent the "middle" when considering differentiation of instruction, educators must acknowledge the variety within this group. Some of these learners may be eligible for basic skills support or may have literacy or math skills that are considered below their grade level. Other learners may excel in certain content areas but may not qualify for enrichment services. Learners who have exited ESL (English as a second language) programs or who no longer are eligible for IEPs or 504 plans are also considered general education learners—as are learners whose parents refuse services.

As we educators now understand that diversity is the norm, we see that the general education learners are an excellent representation of this. With this mindset, we reflect on each activity, lesson, and assessment through the lens of accessibility for all learners.

*"The most important thing in terms of teaching is making sure students feel a sense of community and belonging in the class and the school. They need to feel safe and wanted. While some people feel that this isn't a quality use of our time and that this is less important than content, I disagree. Academics will progress from there."*

—Lauren, supervisor, New Jersey

## Learners Who Have Eligibility for More Than One Set of Services

Just because a learner belongs to one of these subgroups of learners (perhaps being eligible for an ESL program), it doesn't mean that they automatically should not be considered for other services. These learners may be called *twice exceptional* (or dually exceptional). This can be very tricky to navigate because some educators may not have a true understanding of the unique and diverse needs of learners. For example, a learner with an IEP or a behavior plan also may benefit from an enrichment or gifted curriculum. A multilingual learner may have a 504 plan for a medical diagnosis. How about a multilingual learner with an IEP related to her autism diagnosis who belonged in a gifted class for math?

While there are many learners who are twice exceptional, teachers really must ensure two things:

1. Do not recommend a student for an evaluation because of your preconceptions about other subgroups that may describe their strengths or challenges. For example, we wouldn't want to deny an evaluation to a gifted learner or a multilingual learner because their unique needs may not fit our prescribed narrative. (*"He's only been in the country for two years. It's a language issue, not a special-education issue." "This kid is gifted. She doesn't have struggles that may warrant support from an IEP or 504."*)
2. Avoid over-classify learners who may just need time and the right interventions. Some learners may not be working on grade level or may have literacy skills associated with a younger child—for a variety of reasons. However, we cannot mistake lack of opportunity in education with a learning disability. We also must consider the stages of language acquisition that may be masquerading as learning disabilities: a silent period, long processing times, difficulty following multi-step instructions.

Finally, when coordinating different services that learners may receive, it is crucial to put the needs of the learners above all else. These services may include access to a special educator, English support, speech, physical therapy, intense literacy intervention, and other supports. There are only a certain number of hours in the day, however, and the organization and planning of these types of services may be challenging. A commonly cited saying from the past asserted that "special ed trumps everything else" in terms of scheduling services. We now embrace the idea that our learners are entitled to whatever supports and services to which they are eligible—even if that means being creative in terms of scheduling.

## What Is an Inclusion Setting?

> *"The purpose of most of these programs isn't to teach the kids; that's not what is important to them. It's to keep certain kids away from everyone else. It's the opposite of inclusion."*
>
> —Ryan, age 16

In the past, inclusive education solely referred to a classroom model that has enjoyed some controversy over the years. Typically, an "inclusion" class in mainstream education has been a class in which learners who receive special education services are placed alongside their general education peers. There is a classroom or content-area teacher who teaches in this classroom full time. Additionally, one or more certified special education teachers may teach either the full day in this classroom or specific classes at certain times of the day. More recently, teachers of multilingual learners have entered the mix. Paraprofessionals and related service professionals also may serve learners in these classroom settings.

However, districts are now considering different ways to leverage this model to benefit other learners. Shaeffer (2019) maintains that inclusive education goes far beyond the classroom model to consider policies and practices that promote increased retention and attendance rates, celebration of diversity and cohesion among the members of the school community, and reducing inequities in access for learners.

To be clear, inclusion classroom settings across the board are not ideal for all learners. Placement decisions for all learners must consider the LRE (least restrictive environment) in which they can be successful academically and behaviorally. There are some learners who need academic intervention beyond what is provided in an inclusion classroom as noted in their IEP, and they may spend part of the day in a resource room (RR) setting. Other learners may be assigned placement in a self-contained classroom for the most intense interventions and supports and may only be alongside their general education peers for elective courses or specials.

Even though there are times in which the most appropriate placement for some learners is not in an inclusion classroom, educators must strive to provide opportunities for these learners to interact with their peers in creative ways. This may happen during project-based learning where learners from a self-contained class join their peers in their classroom with the support of their teachers and paraprofessionals. Examples of this can include the following:

- Read alouds
- Partner reading
- Virtual field trips
- Working in small groups

Related service professionals may additionally engage their learners with general education peers in "lunch bunch" groups or even support connections in unstructured time. With this in mind, we must extend the typical definition of inclusion to ways beyond the classroom for *all* learners.

Scheduling for inclusion of all classrooms must be deliberate and intentional in terms of ways for all learners to be integrated within the school community. If a learner must participate in certain programs to support academic or behavioral needs, then specific effort must be made to provide opportunities for them to feel included in the community in other ways.

## Conclusion

Inclusion for learners with diverse needs may look different for every learner. For some, this may be the amount of time they spend in a general education classroom. In other instances, this may be access to recess and integration in the cafeteria with age-similar peers. The least restrictive environment may mean much more than academic environments for many learners—and that is where educators must think creatively to foster a sense of belonging in the school community.

## DISCUSSION QUESTIONS

- In which ways can learners be *diverse*? In which ways may diversity be considered positive, and how is it sometimes considered to be a challenge or something negative?
- What is your experience with diversity in your own lifetime—as a student, an educator, and as a human?
- What does access mean in a classroom setting? What does it mean at a school or district level?

# ENGLISH LEARNERS AND MULTILINGUAL LEARNERS

CHAPTER 7

## Frontloaded Vocabulary

**language proficiency:** This refers to the level at which someone may listen, speak, read, and write in a language. It is often measured by a language assessment, and the language proficiency level is often called a way to understand more about a learner's educational needs.

**translanguaging:** Translanguaging refers to the seamless interweaving of any or all languages that any person may have in their repertoire. We may see this as learners who produce language (oral or written) that appears to include more than one language in any given sentence, utterance, conversation, or idea. While some people view this as primarily something that language learners may utilize, this is a staple of multilingual communities and cultures.

As educators, many of us will encounter learners who come from different cultures or speak a variety of languages beyond English. We may share these languages with our learners—or perhaps we do not. Some of these learners have proficiency in English along with these other languages, and others do not yet have the ability to speak English fluently. This chapter is designed to empower ourselves to meet the unique needs of these multilingual learners (MLs) and to celebrate the beautiful diversity that these learners bring to our schools and communities.

## The Many Faces of Multilingual Learners

Learners who are currently learning English have commonly been called *English learners* (ELs) or *English language learners* (ELLs), and in many places, this is the "official" or legal term for learners who are eligible for *English as a second language* (ESL) or *English language development* (ELD) services. There is a movement in our field, however, to designate them in what many educators feel is a more inclusive term that celebrates the additive process of language acquisition: *multilingual learners* or MLs (Furlong, 2022a). Rather than the language acquisition focus bcing solcly on English, this movement embraces that speakers of more than one language should be building up their linguistic repertoire in all their languages throughout their lives. In other words, the "end goal" for these learners is not *only* proficiency in English; rather, we are providing space for them to progress in all their languages. Celebrating multilingualism does not mean that we are teaching them in their other languages (unless these learners are in a bilingual or dual language program), but we value them and allow them to think and express themselves how they feel most empowered.

> *"It is important to acknowledge that multilingual learners have more knowledge and understanding than they may have the English proficiency to express. Consider the things in your own life that you know a lot about; if you were to have to express these things in a language that you don't know, you most certainly may appear that you know very little. For example, I'm a pretty bright person but if you test me in Mandarin, I don't know anything!"*
>
> —Marco

Some of your multilingual learners may come to your class from a different country. Others were born in the country or even possibly the town or city in which you teach. Depending on your community, many younger learners may have been born here and enter our schools speaking the language of their family. It's possible that school may be the first place that they have consistent exposure to English. These very young learners are *dual-language learners* (DLLs), as it is acknowledged that they are simultaneously learning language and literacy in both their dominant (home) language and English.

### EXPERIENCED MULTILINGUALS (FORMERLY LONG-TERM ENGLISH LEARNERS)

As we consider multilingual learners who are eligible for ESL services in older grades, the percentage who have come to us from another country may increase. This may be because our DLLs and learners who were previously eligible for services have gained the proficiency to exit the program. Those who haven't, however, are sometimes referred to as LTELs or LTEMs (*long-term English learners or emergent multilinguals*). While this should not be an issue, this label often carries some negative connotation to it. Educators often feel that there is a time limit that should apply to those who are acquiring additional languages; anyone who doesn't fit that artificial construct is considered not to meet their expectations. According to Huynh and Skelton (2023), a more appropriate term to refer to these learners would be *experienced multilinguals*, as it reframes the focus to a positive aspect of the learners' language journeys.

> *"I have worked with many (monolingual) educators who seemed to feel that they are experts in the field of language acquisition. There is a predetermined amount of time that many believe is the 'cutoff' in terms of what is appropriate for learning an additional language. After this time, educators often ask why this learner still requires ESL services or feel that a learner must have a learning disability if they haven't passed the assessment to exit the program. My feeling is that learning a language is challenging for most people, some more than others. There are many variables that influence a person's path to multilingualism—and we can't assume there is something 'wrong' when it doesn't follow an arbitrary timeline."*
>
> —Denise, teacher educator and author, New Jersey

## MULTILINGUALS WITH EDUCATIONAL DIFFERENCES (STUDENTS WITH LIMITED OR INTERRUPTED EDUCATION)

Another group of multilingual learners who have very specific needs is SLIFE (*students with limited or interrupted education*). The identification of these learners varies from state to state—and many criteria have changed post-pandemic—but these students are multilingual learners who have missed significant time in school either in their home countries or in consideration of their journeys to their new country (Furlong, 2022b). They may arrive at our schools with few academic skills or on an academic level usually associated with a much younger learner. However, there are some very important truths to keep in mind when working with SLIFE:

1. All people—including SLIFE—have learned their entire lives. While sometimes this education may not have been a "traditional" one in what we consider to be a typical classroom, life experiences provide a valuable tool for learning.

2. While these learners may need to learn academic skills that are typically associated with younger learners, we must ensure that we provide that instruction with dignity. The materials, the strategies, and the interactions must all be age relevant and appropriate. No middle schooler should be using the same materials as a first grader—even if they are working on similar skills.
3. Lack of educational opportunity does not equal a learning disability. While it is certainly not impossible that these learners may have a learning disability, please know that their challenges and rate of learning may be a result of their educational experiences. Time and appropriate instruction are crucial—and it is the responsibility of the school district to meet the unique needs of these learners.

Important to note is that there are debates and discussions about the inherent negativity in this *label* for learners—which is where the problems with categorizing human beings arise. Labels are useful in terms of providing information about the needs and strengths of learners; they should not be considered something that holds any learner back from exceeding any expectations. As traditional deficit-based language is being reexamined in the field, SLIFE should be reconsidered as well. One option is to focus on neutral to positive perspectives, such as MEDs (*multilinguals with educational differences*).

Although multilingual learners most certainly have a variety of needs that span the spectrum of educational services, it is important for all educators to understand that they can learn, will learn, and are people from whom we all should learn.

## The Needs of Multilingual Learners

Our learners deserve an entire community who is knowledgable of their various cultures, languages, strengths, and challenges. All members of this community (administrators, teachers, guidance counselors, child study team members, office representatives, paraprofessionals, custodial staff, lunch assistants) must be trained in representative and connective pedagogy to best support the unique needs of all learners. In other words, being culturally responsive and sustaining is an effort that may be led by the ESL staff but must be consistent across the entire school community. More on Culturally Responsive Teaching in Chapter 8.

> *"Multilingual learners may not always understand what you're saying when they first arrive, but they do know the meaning of a warm smile. It's important to establish with them that you are happy they are there."*
>
> —Veronica, high school EL/ML teacher, New Jersey

First and foremost, all learners need a school and classroom community in which they are welcomed and their differences are celebrated. This is evidenced by the physical environment and sense of belonging for all children and adults. Everyone in these classrooms are language learners, and all people are open to learning and making mistakes in a safe space. Once this is established, teachers should build on this environment in other ways, such as the following:

1. **Providing access to curricula that are grade-level relevant yet at the academic level that is relevant to their needs.** Just because a learner may not have a high level of proficiency in English (yet), that doesn't mean that they should not engage in the same content and learning standards as their peers.
2. **Investing in building background.** Sometimes MLs have not studied the same content in their past education as our other learners. Using videos, visuals, word walls, interactive learning, and collaboration are all ways to help build the foundational knowledge.
3. **Providing access to gifted and talented (G&T) or enrichment services.** Criteria should consider multiple measures to ensure access. Often standardized scores are a main factor in determining eligibility for G&T; however, there should be other considerations for learners who may have talents that are not measured in that fashion. Challenges in scheduling must not preclude opportunities for any learner who is determined to be eligible—regardless of English proficiency.
4. **Representing their cultures and experiences in literature and curricula.** "Culturally responsive teaching leverages students' linguistic and cultural backgrounds" (Snyder & Fenner, 2021, p. 200). Learners must not only "see" themselves in what they are reading and learning, they must also experience their cultures and languages presented in a positive light. More on Culturally Responsive Teaching in Chapter 8.
5. **Providing SEMH (social-emotional mental health) support for traumatic experiences.** While we teachers

are not mental-health experts, there are ways we can be supportive for our learners that are well within our roles. These include being sensitive and proactive to things that may be anxiety-producing for students, such as emergency drills or even speaking in front of the class (Furlong, 2022b).

6. **Acknowledging that some behaviors and anxieties may come from places that we as educators may not understand.** We should not jump to conclusions about our learners based on behaviors that may be signs of traumatic experiences. Remembering that it "takes a village" to educate any child (or something like that!) is important. Reach out to specialists in your district to get as much help for these learners as possible. Guidance counselors, school psychologists, administrators, and social workers may know resources that may assist families that we teachers never knew.

7. **Having a growth mindset.** We educators live in the world of *yet*. While our learners may not *yet* have the proficiency in multiple languages that they soon will, we walk alongside them in their educational journey toward their goals. Many people consider multilingualism in a native English speaker to be an asset but have a much more judgmental view of our learners who are learning English. Teachers must shift this mindset, as these learners are our future—just as much as other groups of children.

8. **Embracing getting discouraged as part of the journey.** Embracing the journey, the goals, and the anticipated outcome can help them keep their "eye on the prize." Engaging our MLs in peer leadership, student council, and being captains of sports teams are powerful ways to foster those relationships and senses of belonging. Often these learners are overlooked though their voice and perspective are so valuable within the school community.

9. **Providing opportunities for MLs to engage in extracurricular activities, such as art and sports.** This will give them chances to connect with their peers in a less formal way and over their mutual interests.

10. **Allowing space for home-school connections.** All communications sent home from the school must represent the home languages of all learners and their families. Opportunities for translators for all meetings and conferences must be available. Sometimes parents do not regularly use email. Finding technology for communication (many offer translations!) that work for your learners' families is key. Comments such as "Those parents never come to conferences!" may ignore the struggles and

challenges that our learners' families may be facing. Avoid judgment and focus on outreach.

11. **Providing support for their needs outside of academics.** Learners may need support in accessing services to which they may be eligible through the school, such as free or reduced-cost lunch, backpack programs, or healthcare programs. Connecting our learners to resources in the community (outreach organizations, sports clubs, homework help, childcare resources) may help these families build their community of support.

When the school community is one in which *all* stakeholders are learners about other cultures and languages, curiosity about and conversations that support true appreciation for diversity become the norm. Everyone benefits from this culture and environment.

## The Role of Their Heritage/Dominant Language

*"Yes, we now have so many types of technology that we can use to engage our MLs in their heritage languages. This is fantastic—if we don't consider that our only tool in our toolbox. It's so important that we keep the individual needs of our learners in mind as we plan for scaffolds and supports. I have worked with MLs who get frustrated by everything being translated and others who feel that they need to leverage their heritage language to learn the content at that time. Also, some of our students may have had limited access to technology and we cannot assume that they can pick up and work independently on the laptops. The trick is to provide different levels of supports to keep access at the forefront."*

—Rose, educator, Pennsylvania

It's important to begin this section with the following: The use of heritage to build background knowledge is useful and highly encouraged for a variety of reasons, but there is more to engaging these learners in learning than translating all content. This is sometimes the "go-to" or only accommodation educators make for MLs, and it is *sometimes not the best practice.* There are many ways we must engage our MLs in content areas, and providing scaffolding in the heritage languages is only one of them.

If our MLs have strong literacy skills in their heritage language, we may sometimes provide them with videos, paragraphs, and vocabulary engagement that includes their language—whether we as the teacher speak it. Teachers can use videos with subtitles in any language or even screencasts that allow us to speak in English over some short, translated material. You can present new content vocabulary in English with visuals or other explanations instead of translating—but sometimes creating those connections to prior knowledge may be helpful. With technology, translations may not be perfect, but if we can use heritage languages to build some schema (background knowledge) for our learners, it is appropriate. Multilingual word walls are a great way to engage learners as well—learners can even participate in creating them!

To be clear, our goal in educating MLs is more than specifically targeting English acquisition; we do want to leverage *all* our learners' languages as they are learning. Leveraging all languages in our learners' individual repertoires is crucial both academically and social-emotionally. However, as we are teaching content at the given grade level, simply translating may not give our learners the information and background they need to truly understand. As our learners are currently in this grade, they may not have seen this vocabulary nor these concepts before, so the words in their heritage language may not mean much to them.

When our learners are *receiving* information from us through reading or listening, we can engage them in a way that provides them with multisensory experiences with content and vocabulary. They can *see* visuals, anchor charts, word walls, vocabulary lists, primary sources, and videos. They can *hear* recordings, songs, lessons, repeated use of words, books/passages read aloud, and use of language. They can *touch* models, globes, artifacts, and realia. *Smelling* and *tasting* may be less common but can certainly be parts of specific lessons.

As our learners are *producing* language, they have many ways in which they can communicate their understanding or share their voices. We have established that our multilingual learners most certainly have much more knowledge, understanding, opinion, and voice than they may have the English to express themselves. Their knowledge base is incredible and certainly may be far beyond their proficiency in English—and this doesn't mean that they should not use whatever languages they like to engage in communication and learning.

*"Studying World War I was complicated for my Korean students, as not only was the language very different from their home language, but also the content itself was culturally very far away from theirs. Luckily, one of the ELA teachers was Korean, and she was happy to share with me one documentary in Korean that these students could watch to understand the concepts and events that we were studying in class. I asked my Korean students to come up with a list of keywords that they*

*considered important to understand the unit, and I copied them in big adhesive notes with a visual by each of them. Then, they translated the word into the same adhesive paper, and we created an anchor chart that we placed right by the whiteboard. This way, they could easily look at the words while I was explaining. I also allowed them to have content related discussions in Korean. Every time I suggested that they could have access to materials in their home language, or create material, or use it to better understand the content, their facial expressions just relaxed and they smiled!"*

—Marta, EL educator, Germany

## TRANSLANGUAGING

One way our learners can use all their languages in communication is through translanguaging. As explained at the start of this chapter, translanguaging practices are authentic ways that humans utilize all the languages in their repertoire to effectively communicate. Languages do not exist alone in one's brain; therefore, it makes sense that one may leverage what they know in all their languages as they engage with others.

Translanguaging may be used and embraced in many ways, one of which may be the product of language spanning different languages. For example, our learner may start a sentence in their heritage language and complete it in another language—or two or three.

Alliteration is when a writer uses *os mesmos sons* [the same sounds] to begin many words in *um poema* [a poem], *uma caçào* [a song], or other types of writing or speaking. (Portuguese)

My family and I visited *Stare Miasto* [Old Town] in Poland, a historic part of Gdańsk, and saw the beautiful *katedra* [cathedral]. (Polish)

In my country, I studied *wiskunde* [math] with *my onderwyser* [my teacher] and I got good grades. (Afrikaans)

With these examples, one may see that learners sometimes express certain features of language in their heritage languages. This may be because they have not yet learned the vocabulary in English, or it may be that there are connections or connotations to the words in their heritage languages. This allows our learners to express what they can or want in the target language while also utilizing other languages to complete their thoughts. Empowering our learners to use all their languages in their verbal or written communication is a platform for them to make sense of language and celebrate their own multilingualism.

Translanguaging is a valid form of expression—no matter the stage of language acquisition. Learners can use whatever English they have acquired as they are producing language and communicate the rest of their ideas in their dominant language—in writing or speaking. They may even write their responses or answers first and then go back and add key words in English. People who are fluent in all their languages may still use translanguaging as they communicate as a way of expressing belonging to a group of multilinguals or because certain words in languages have specific connotations that they appreciate.

But what happens when teachers do not understand the languages that their learners are producing?

> *"Embracing the beauty of multilingualism can help students overcome the apprehension of grappling with unfamiliar languages, especially when they're limited to using only English in the classroom. I vividly recall my time as an administrator, a role that constantly presented me with the challenge of fostering open-mindedness by my staff to allow students to use Arabic, their first language, in class. I would often find myself encouraging teachers to shed their fear of not comprehending what students were talking about in Arabic. I shared my personal journey of learning to appreciate the nuances of multilingualism. Just as I had to learn to decipher the unspoken cues of my students' body language to gauge their engagement, I realized that the essence of communication extended beyond verbal expressions. I explained to my team that some students needed to use their first language to help them acquire English. We didn't have to understand Arabic to know whether they were on task or not. In most cases, if lessons were interesting and students were involved, they only communicated in Arabic to ensure they understood the content and/or directions."*
>
> —Ilene, educator and author, Kuwait

Ensuring that our multilingual learners understand that we value all their languages and there is honored space for their unique language repertoires in our collective language journeys is crucial to the culture that builds up our learners rather than views them from a deficit perspective.

## Being Culturally Responsive to All Learners

Never correct a learner who is speaking in another language to speak in "*English only, please!*" As learners gain proficiency in English, it may be appropriate within class to ask them to increase their use of English in assignments, but refusing the opportunity to communicate in a learner's dominant language is damaging to their perception of themselves. Period.

Languages and cultures are integral parts of a learner's backpack of experiences and identity. Valuing differences here shows that you value the learner. Consider the mental exhaustion that our learners may experience when communicating in a language in which they are not yet proficient. Interactions in the lunchroom or hallways should always be in the language of choice if there are others who share that language. Incidentally, a beautiful by-product of this may be that learners are learning even more languages than their own (and English) so they can forge these relationships with other multilingual learners! These are authentic interactions and connections that are so powerful in fostering senses of belonging for *all* learners.

Opportunities to listen to music or other ways to hear one's heritage language should also be permitted during these unstructured times if desired. This may be over the loudspeaker as learners are entering or exiting the school or even during lunch or in gym or art class. As there may be several languages represented in a school, there are many opportunities for all learners to be exposed to music and culture from around the world.

> *"I first came to my school when it was Hispanic Heritage Month, not that I understood this. I was so happy because I heard things about my country and the school talked about artists and music that I knew. I did not realize then that this would end soon, and it would be unusual to hear my language or see my culture in the school. Until next year. As a teacher now, I remember this and make sure I think about how my students would like to see themselves."*
>
> —Carlos Ángel

By intentionally creating an environment within the school and district that celebrates differences, all stakeholders feel seen and included. These stakeholders are learners, families, teachers, staff, administration, and community members. Not only do they feel pride and connections when their own cultures are celebrated, but gaining understanding and appreciation for others' cultures is empowering as well.

Some strategies that can be implemented include the following:

- Morning announcements and greetings in different languages are great ways to create a structured and predictable way to engage in learning about community cultures.
  - By reciting the date and weather in English and rotating the languages of the community, schools integrate small

opportunities to expose all learners to various languages. Multilingual learners will also hear non-native speakers of their language attempting to communicate, which can be a powerful way to experience their languages.

  - Programs in which languages of the community are highlighted may promote small interactions in different languages, such as greetings. Initiatives encouraging learners to become "global travelers" and focus on different countries or languages for a week may be a great way to provide language exposure and respect. These weeks may be paired with fun facts about the country with the morning announcements. (*Did you know that Turkey is the only country to span two continents? Did you know that in Uruguay there are more sheep than people?*)

- Signage and bulletin boards that represent cultures beyond "special months" will establish appreciation for diversity as an integral part of the community. Some educators create bulletin boards that highlight languages or countries and others may focus on contributions of people with diverse backgrounds. Displaying student work is also a great way to share the voices of different learners.
- Assemblies, events, and activities are also special ways to engage as a community in lifting up cultures. Most effective may be actual voices from the community who would like to share things that they value or that represent them. These may be grand events or as simple as read alouds from parents or art projects that connect to traditions of the community.
- Acknowledgment when current events happen in home countries is so important to showing empathy and understanding for those who may be worried about loved ones far away. With younger learners, communication with families would be necessary first to ensure they aren't learning of these things for the first time in class, but older students may appreciate the acknowledgment of the importance of global happenings.

We will cover more on Culturally Responsive Teaching in Chapter 8.

## Conclusion

As an educator, it may sometimes be easy to fall into a trap of focusing on what you perceive your students cannot do as ways to define them. (*They can't speak a word of English! They've never learned anything like what we're doing, and I just don't see how they can keep up. I don't know their names; they are the ELD teacher's students. Not knowing English is a disability in history class.*)

Even if these types of statements may seem cruel or judgmental, these are actual things teachers have said to me [Denise] in the past few years. To be clear, multilingual learners are capable of learning and contributing to the class and school community.

All educators in communities in which there are multilingual learners are part of their educational journey. Whether or not educators have multilingual learners in their classes, it is everyone's responsibility to support them and include them in the school culture. Multilingual learners bring beautiful opportunities for us to learn about the world through a different lens. A smile in the hallway or an acknowledgment of small successes are so important to support them on their journeys.

As you can see, *if you know one multilingual learner . . . you know* one *multilingual learner.* The important thing is to keep an open mind and truly believe in your heart that these learners are valuable to your classroom community and that they *will* succeed!

## DISCUSSION QUESTIONS

- What are some rules or guidelines that would be relevant to educating learners who do not yet have strong proficiency in English?
- What needs do you see in your EL/ML students that are outside of academics or language acquisition? How can you meet those needs?

# DYNAMIC AND RESPONSIVE LEARNING

CHAPTER 8

## Frontloaded Vocabulary

**modifications:** Modify means "change." These are changes that educators make to activities, assessments, and the curriculum to provide access for learners with diverse needs.

**accommodations:** These are changes in the ways that learners access the activities, assessments, and the curriculum—but are not changes to the actual task.

**points of access:** These are ways that educators consider providing connections between the learners they serve and the content/skills/literature/language they are learning.

**self-efficacy:** Positive self-efficacy is when a person believes that they are capable of completing a goal or accomplishing a task. ●

Responsive teaching may be difficult to explicitly identify—as it changes for the individual needs of our learners. True responsive educators may never be the ones who claim to be experts at it, rather, they constantly check themselves and their biases to ensure they are on the right track on any given day or lesson.

> *"When I say that I 'learn alongside' my students, I don't mean that I am learning fifth-grade math with them. I mean that my constant reflections of my own biases and my perceptions help me to learn about myself, my students, my teaching, and the world we live in. I want to know ways to grow, both as an educator and as a human. And these are things I learn from my students, their families, my colleagues, and the community where I teach."*
>
> —Denise, teacher educator and author, New Jersey

In *Culturally Responsive Teaching and the Brain*, Hammond (2016) connects Vygotsky's work with culturally responsive teaching and how engaging learners in collaboration fosters cultural connections and collectivist principles. She advises that educators must acknowledge that *culturally responsive teaching* is not a set of strategies or a specific program to be adopted, rather, it is a mindset that must color everything educators do. Even though culture is referenced in the name of this mindset, Hammond's work addresses a variety of ways that learners may have diverse needs and how we as educators can make *how* they learn (not just what they learn!) accessible and meaningful. Perhaps one of the most important aspects of culturally responsive teaching may be the reflective practices of the educators in ways that they can better understand their learners. Educators should ask themselves the following questions when approaching their work and their students:

1. **What are our learners' academic experiences, and how can they leverage those experiences in their learning?** Some of our learners may have challenges in learning certain areas or may have had missed or interrupted education (for a variety of reasons). A learner who attended a homeschooling program or who is entering our schools from another state or country may have learned so much in their education (and life!) experiences, but it is possible that it doesn't align with the expectations of their new schools.
2. **What are cultural, religious, health-related, and linguistic factors that impact learners' experiences in school?** Learners who do not celebrate holidays (such as Halloween) may experience feelings of being left out or different in a negative way if their teachers do not understand ways to design their classroom activities in a more inclusive way. These are particularly important in the younger grades as holidays are sometimes part of the curriculum. Points of access to all activities that consider all health- and physical-related differences must also drive all educational decisions. Considering the diverse needs of learners in everything we do is critical to fostering feelings of belonging.

3. **How do we build on strengths and support where there are challenges in learning?** It's crucial to acknowledge that all learners have areas in which they feel most confident and other areas in which they may need more support. How do our learners' past and current experiences influence their education, relationships, and lives outside of school? Educators must focus on celebrating and leveraging strengths while boosting their learners' skills and language when needed.

4. **How do different cultures define success?** This is where we teachers must really consider our own bias and experiences from an objective point of view. How does our specific culture measure success in adults and what is the measure for learners? Are our expectations for success shifted for different groups of people? If educators are seeking to have high expectations for all learners, how are they determined and are they accessible to all?

*"One of the first things I learned as a new teacher was to build relationships with your students and learn about them and what interests them. It makes a huge difference to have that connection with them and it'll make difficult conversations easier to have if they are necessary."*

—Matt, educator and coach, New Jersey

## Collaboration

When considering ways to provide learners opportunities in learning through collaboration, there are many pathways for engagement. Sometimes groups are *heterogeneous* (representing differences among learners), and other times they may be *homogeneous* (learners with similar interests, proficiencies, strengths). Teachers may set up these groups intentionally, randomly, or they may allow learners to choose with whom they work. The design and structure of the group depends on the activity and assessment and should be chosen accordingly.

As educators consider these different models of intentional grouping for collaboration, they often refer to the work of Vygosky and *sociocultural theory* (SCT) (Cherry, 2023). Within SCT, Vygotsky analyzed how people learn and the impact one's interactions with others may have on how one progresses. If learners perform tasks or solve problems alongside someone who is more proficient in that area (Vygotsky's term is the *more knowledgeable other* or MKO). This type of learning may take on many different looks in our classrooms depending upon the activity, the goals of the activity, the assessments, and the individual learners.

## COLLABORATIVE LEARNING GROUPS

*Collaborative learning groups* are great ways to engage all students in low-stress language production while also working on content-area concepts. Low-stakes opportunities to produce language are critical! Valuing the voice of all students boosts their confidence and feelings of self-efficacy and self-worth.

If teachers use this type of group, they should keep in mind the following guidelines:

1. **Groups must be dynamic, not static.** Educators must change groups for different activities or content areas to increase the amount of interaction learners have with different students. These classmates then feel more of a connection to one another and may be more likely to include one another in activities outside the classroom (recess, cafeteria, gym). Groups that change often also prevent the notions that learners may have about the "smart" group or the "slow" group that may accompany internalization of what those perceptions may mean for them.
2. **Establishing norms and structure is key to successful collaborative group work.** Some sample norms that could be helpful include the following:
    - All learners must respect the contributions of everyone.
    - All learners must contribute in some fashion.
    - All learners must stay on task.
    - Contributions from various learners may look different, but all are valuable.
    - All learners must help and encourage one another. Stay positive!
3. **All group members must have an assignment appropriate to their level of language proficiency and content knowledge.** However, our learners with diverse needs should not always do the "drawing" section or the easiest. Equitable distribution of responsibility is critical to all learners feeling empowered and like an important part of the group. We want all learners to feel that they are an integral part of any team.
4. **The goals of collaborative learning must be established as the *journey* rather than always the product.** This will articulate to all learners that the strongest participant cannot just get everything done so it's right—all contributions are valuable and part of the feedback at the end of the activity. The authenticity of the activities is also an important part of the journey; we don't have group work simply for the sake of checking off a box.

5. **No one in these groups should be presented as the *expert*, and no one is the *novice*.** Everyone is learning at levels that are relevant to their unique needs, and everyone is moving forward. All contributions are valuable. If learners are working with peers who may have higher proficiency in English or a more developed reading level, these peers should not take the place of the teacher. Instruction is the responsibility of the educator, and "bilingual buddies" or "high-level peers" must not be given tasks that take on that role.
6. **Students may have different values and experiences with working collaboratively, and educators must support them as they navigate new forums for learning.** Considering learners with diverse needs, they have opportunities to produce language and content in a small group rather than as a member of an *audience* in a whole-group lesson.

The most important thing to remember about collaborative learning groups is that the structure and purpose must be authentic for the learning to be meaningful. For example, learners who may have attentional challenges can find this change of space and modality of learning a great way to keep them engaged. The structure of specific roles and expectations that are clear and communicated are also critical to the success of these (and all!) learners. Providing learners the opportunities to work together in this way can help create stakeholders in the success of all peers in class. Learners may learn alongside peers whom they may not otherwise have the chance to know well, especially with heterogeneous groups. Those connections may transcend the walls of the classroom into the cafeteria, recess areas, and possibly even future years in school. Consider these activities as opportunities for your learners to build their skills and connections at the same time.

## Learning Styles and Strengths

Gardner's multiple intelligence theory (Gardner, 1983, 1987, as noted by Ruhl, 2023) has been a common way to explain learning styles and strengths through descriptions of eight types of intelligences: interpersonal, linguistic, intrapersonal, naturalistic, spatial, existential, musical, and logical-mathematical. While most educators embrace the notion that learners acquire knowledge in different ways, some academics have moved away from this theory as it does not account for other forms of "intelligence," nor has it been empirically tested (Ruhl, 2023). Instead, teachers should focus on ways we can engage our learners' *strengths* in different ways.

## DIFFERENT MODALITIES

One of the ways we account for the different strengths of our learners would be to provide opportunities to engage in content in different modalities. This may allow learners to experience learning in different ways and process information through their various senses. Consider using choice boards for both activities and assessments in ways that provide chances for learners to work to their strengths and interests. Within these choices, learners can demonstrate understanding of the language, skills, and concepts of the unit in ways that give them feelings of agency and motivation.

Some of our learners feel strong connections to music and may process information more effectively through song, poetry, and rhyme. While we see this very often when working with our very youngest learners, this is often still very engaging with our middle and high schoolers. I have seen collaborative groups writing rap songs to science concepts and singing and line dancing as they recall events in history.

Multisensory literacy instruction considers the different ways we process information through various modalities as well. Learners connect written symbols to verbal sounds and movements. They also sometimes "write" using their fingers in shaving cream, sand, or even on sandpaper. Song and rhythm are also used to engage learners in learning foundational language and literacy skills.

## PROVIDING CHOICE

Gardner's work also includes interpersonal and intrapersonal strengths (Ruhl, 2023). As we encourage collaboration and group work as something valued in our society, we must also acknowledge that interpersonal work is not the preferred way for all learners to learn all the time. Giving choice in this respect (to work with peers or alone) may be responsive to the needs of some of your learners.

Variations of assessments acknowledge that learners may know more about a topic or skill than they have the language to express in a certain way. Providing a low-stress way (and choice!) in which learners can use multiple modalities to engage in assessments is crucial to feelings of self-efficacy.

For example, across all classes, learners will likely be asked to demonstrate some type of *claim, evidence and reasoning* (CER). In ELA, this might be in the form of an essay, in math, by showing their work and explaining how they reached their answer, in science, by conducting an experiment, and so on. Consider and allow student to approach their CER in ways that make sense for them while still adhering to the request to show all three components of the task:

1. ELA and history:
   a. Some learners will write an essay without any scaffolds or supports. These learners may also *extend past the prompt* and research other historical mysteries to which they can compare this one. This would possibly be learners who show strengths in these areas (writing, history, analysis), and it is important to consider ways to meet their diverse needs as well.
   b. Others may need a *graphic organizer* or possibly even an outline of the information to help break down the details and then write an essay. Breaking topics and information into digestible chunks may be exactly what learners who have challenges with executive functioning would need. The end product may look similar to those who go straight to the essay, but the steps provide scaffolding to support learners in arriving at that point.
   c. Some might need the scaffolds along with *stems or frames* that help them craft their sentences or paragraphs. These samples that support the use of language may empower multilingual learners or learners who have challenges in written language production. The end product may look similar to the essays of their peers, or it may appear more like an *annotated outline*—whichever best fits the goals of the assignment and strengths of the learners.
   d. Multilingual learners may *translanguage* (use more than one language) within their response and may use any or none of these scaffolds. MLs may also benefit from resources that either clarify the evidence/information in their heritage language or in *comprehensible English*. While many learners in this class may have little schema on this topic, we must also be respectful and curious about what our learners who may have attended school in other places may have learned.
2. In math, science or social studies:
   a. Learners who feel that they have strengths in the visual-spatial realm may create an *artifact* in which they can detail the evidence that supports their claim. These visuals may contain complete sentences, phrases, or single-word utterances and may accompany a shortened version of the essay. Learners may create this using technology, a trifold, poster board, or through a three-dimensional modality (like a diorama).
   b. Learners may *draw* a representation of their claim with details that represent the evidence. If possible, they may label parts of their drawing with a word bank or other

resources if necessary. This may also take the form of a hand-written or electronic comic strip. Drawing is a valid form of expression for language learners who cannot yet easily write, no matter their age. Supplementing the writing with some words or sounds—or verbally describing it—can be a way to interact with language in a productive way. For many, the step of drawing may help clarify concepts in their minds before they begin their writing process. This may benefit learners who have challenges in reading or writing for a variety of reasons, learners with attentional issues, or multilingual learners. Creating short picture books designed to build schema on this event may also be a great way to engage all learners in different ways.

3. In art (visual and performing):
   a. Some learners may benefit from the opportunity to share their work *verbally*. This may be a video, a dialogue with a peer, or a planned conference with a teacher. A relevant option for this project may be to report the information as if they were journalists. If writing is what is being assessed, learners can plan out notes of what they will present/share, and this can be included as part of the assessment.
   b. Some learners might want to *act out physically*. Some of the evidence may be a way to engage those learners who have strengths in kinesthetic areas. They may even create a *readers theater* presentation in which information is presented in a collaborative way with levels of language that are appropriate to all learners who participate. This may be an extension project for gifted students or an avenue to provide access for students whose strengths lie in this arena.

Providing choice and expanding beyond the typical realms of assessment and checking for understanding allows both the teacher and the student to share knowledge in a way that is most beneficial and comfortable for them.

## Accessing Content Creatively

As we view everything we do with the learners we serve through a lens of equity and access, we must consistently reflect on how to provide pathways to engagement for all learners. Not everyone is going to learn best with the teacher in the front of the room teaching whole-group lessons. Learners often need various *points of access* for them to truly engage with a lesson.

### VIDEO AND AUDIO RECORDINGS

An example of how we can provide this for our learners may be to support the mini lesson you have in class with an additional screen recording of you explaining the concept with visuals and written words on your screen. Teachers can utilize free screen recording resources for five minutes (we don't want anything longer than that!) to record their voice, share their screen, and review concepts and vocabulary. You may also record a video call session by yourself with your screen being the star of the show. If you can activate subtitles, learners will both see and hear your words. Teachers can then post this to their classroom forum for learners to watch and rewatch if needed. This is especially useful for study guides and help with concepts assigned for homework. For learners to respond, forums like Padlet are great ways to provide space for their voices.

Audiobooks and video recordings that may support learners in accessing literature (poetry, articles, news events) are sometimes a bit controversial. (*How am I going to get him to read if he is only listening to a book?*) However, these access points are crucial in building language and literacy skills and are part of supporting reading and writing progress. Ditto for interactive and scaffolded read alouds—at all grades levels.

### VISUALS IN THE CLASSROOM

Learners may create their own resources that they may use when engaging in writing, reading, and the content areas. I have provided a small notebook for learners in which they can write new words, jot down ideas, comment on cultural differences, and write reminders to themselves. Providing a space in which learners have freedom to create something that meets their unique needs—no matter their age—is a powerful pathway toward ownership in their own learning.

Other visuals include anchor charts that support languages and skills needed for content. Multilingual and/or visual word walls that scaffold academic vocabulary are key. Also, displaying student creativity and work may boost pride in both growth and the physical classroom/school environment. And if they are utilized and referenced meaningfully, they are more than wallpaper.

## Accommodations and Modifications

Many educators use the terms *accommodations* and *modifications* when referencing ways that they include learners with diverse needs, but they may not know the differences between these terms.

*Accommodations* would include ways that we change the pathway to the task or activity—but we do not change the activity itself. Examples of accommodations may include larger print for learners with visual impairments or attentional challenges or use of technology when writing for learners with fine motor issues.

*Modifications* refer to when the task or assessment is changed to meet the unique needs of the learner. These may include fewer test questions for learners who may physically fatigue easily or the use of a calculator for learners who have challenges with foundational math skills.

While educators often consider ways to provide these points of access for learners in their classes, there are protocols that must be considered. Typically, modifications/changes in assignments and assessments would be included in a learner's IEP (*Individualized Education Plan*) that accompanies a special education program. We covered IEPs and more in Chapter 6.

Modifications for *multilingual learners* (MLs) are also often approved by decision makers in terms of reduced items on activities and the use of comprehensible/clearer English. Other than situations like these, modifications on assessments are mainly not approved without discussion with administrators. More on modifications for MLs in Chapter 7.

Accommodations that provide pathways to engagement are a bit more individualized than modifications. Because the tasks are not changed when considering accommodations without modifications, they are often considered part of the differentiation of instruction that may benefit learners with diverse needs.

As we are considering ways to be responsive educators, we do see the learners we serve as more than receptacles of knowledge. We constantly reflect on ways we can pave the paths for them to take charge of their learning and embrace their unique journeys. Modifications and accommodations provide points of access to these journeys, both through an academic lens and as human beings.

## Trauma-Informed Practices and Healing-Centered Engagement

The learners we serve carry their own *backpack of experiences* (Furlong, 2022b) with them throughout their lives. These backpacks include things they have done and seen throughout their lives that shape them. These experiences are both positive and challenging, and they color the lens through which learners see life. These backpacks are how they make sense of the world and may be how they survive. Learners come to sit in our classrooms with life experiences about which we may have no idea.

Educators have their own backpacks as well. In these backpacks, we carry our own educational and life experiences, biases, schema, perspectives, values, assumptions, and so on. In my mind, the things that we carry that bring us peace, understanding, and motivation make our backpacks lighter and help us on our path. We do have other things that may weigh us down, and as educators, it's our responsibility to consistently take inventory of these things to consider if they serve us well or not.

It is widely known that—as frustrating as it may sometimes be—behavior is a form of communication. Williams (2023) discusses the importance of a shift in our mindset when considering how this communication manifests in our schools. When we acknowledge that the learners and families we serve may have lived a thousand lives before entering our world, we can understand that our learners' backpacks may influence the way they learn or the way they interact with others. This doesn't mean that we don't have norms that we uphold in terms of behavior, attendance, and academics; this means that the way we support our learners in meeting these expectations is through a lens of compassion and understanding.

Ginwright (2018) explains that "*trauma-informed care* [emphasis added] broadly refers to a set of principles that guide and direct how we view the impact of severe harm on young people's mental, physical, and emotional health" (p. 1). The U.S. Center for Disease Control and Prevention (as noted by Wisner, 2024) explains that ACEs (*adverse childhood experiences*) may include experiences like the following before a child turns 18:

- Physical or emotional abuse
- Abandonment or neglect
- Loss of a family member to suicide
- Substance abuse or alcoholism in the household
- A mentally ill parent
- An incarcerated parent
- Parental divorce or separation

Wisner (2024) also says that ACEs are common, with over 64% of adults reporting that they have experienced at least one of these (with 17.4% saying that they have gone through four or more of them). Many children who experience one or more ACEs feel symptoms akin to *toxic stress* (Wisner, 2024), with mental, emotional, and physical effects.

In schools, this is when educators focus on holistic views of learners' needs rather than pinpointing behaviors and punishments. This doesn't mean that there are no consequences to actions; the view of these behaviors is taken *within the context* of who the learner is and what supports they may need. Therapy, restorative practices, and mentoring may be included in these support systems.

> *"One of our multilingual learners had the nickname 'The Raging Bull' because of his anger issues. What people didn't realize was the trauma that this kid went through before coming to us. Not only did he not have the language to express himself with these teachers and administrators, he had learned not to trust people and that the best way to communicate his frustrations was physically. People refused to look past the surface of his behaviors to see how they could understand what this kid had gone through to get to this point. In fact, when he had outbursts, no one wanted to deal with him. They just sent him to me, the ESL teacher."*
>
> —Sarah, bilingual educator and parent, New Jersey

As part of our journeys in becoming culturally responsive educators, it is crucial that we understand the cultures and experiences of the learners and families we serve. That doesn't mean that we will know everyone's entire stories; it is up to our learners and their families to decide what they share with us. However, if we do not know specifics, we can be cognizant and respectful of what is happening in our learners' communities and reflective on how these events may impact their lives.

But trauma-informed practices are only part of the equation. Ginwright (2018) quotes one of the young people with whom he worked named Marcus: *"I am more than what happened to me; I'm not just my trauma"* (p. 1). While it is critical that we understand the experiences of these young people without blinders on, we do have to embrace their assets and their potential—and their humanity. This is where we shift to *healing-centered engagement* (HCE). According to Ginwright (2021), there are five principles of HCE (CARMA):

1. *Culture*: It is important to identify and affirm culture through positive conversations and connections.
2. *Agency*: Educators must engage with young people in politics and problem solving within the community and beyond.
3. *Relationships*: Ginwright specifies that we should cultivate relationships beyond our title/role. We should engage with young people in our communities and see them as more than *students* and ourselves as more than *teachers*.

4. *Meaning:* We guide young people as they find their own assets and ways that they will advocate and positively impact their lives.
5. *Aspirations:* This goes beyond conversations about the future; young people must be able to see their influence and potential for change—both currently and throughout their lives.

To be clear, we as educators in the classroom cannot take on every role in a young person's life. We engage with colleagues in our districts, in our communities, and even long-distance resources to best support the learners we serve in a responsive way.

## Strengthening Bonds With Families and Communities

When we consider responsive learning environments, it is crucial to think about connections with the families of our learners. Educators at times find it easy to pass judgment on parents and have strong opinions on how they *should* support their children. While we consider ourselves to be educators of the learners we serve, we would be very short-sighted if we did not acknowledge the impact of our relationships with their families on their education. Consider the following tips in this section.

### TIP 1: REMEMBER THAT *ALL* PARENTS WANT TO HELP

Some parents want to support the education of their children but are unsure how to best do that. This may be because they struggled in school themselves or are unfamiliar with the school system in your town (or in the United States). Others may—for a variety of reasons—have limited literacy skills either in English or in their heritage language. There are also times in which parents' views of school were negative and the interactions that they still have on behalf of their children are influenced by these experiences. Also, let's face it: It's not easy to teach and it's also not easy to help with homework, sometimes even under the best of circumstances.

### TIP 2: CULTURAL DIFFERENCES AROUND EXPECTATIONS MAY BE AT PLAY

Sometimes, cultural differences concerning school affect how involved the families of our students may be. In some cultures, there is a separation between family responsibilities and school responsibilities. Some families feel that the "teacher knows best" and that they are being respectful of the knowledge of educators when they stay out of issues related to school. Additionally, in some cultures, school norms are very different than ours in the United States, and parents may find them difficult or new to navigate.

## TIP 3: ASSUME THE BEST INTENTIONS OF FAMILIES AND PARENTS

We as educators must understand that sometimes we only see what may appear to be on the surface. "These parents never come to school events; they must not care." "I've emailed that parent several times and they never even bother to respond. I even translated my message!" "Why don't the parents just ___?" Instead, teachers should *assume the best* in all situations when working with families of all learners. *It is better to be wrong in assuming the best of someone than wrong in assuming the worst.*

Parents may work multiple jobs or different hours, and our learners may be supporting in running the household. We may see effects of this in many different ways. This may be when attendance is an issue; our older learners must miss school when younger siblings are sick or if their parents need support in official matters during the school day. Homework may be a casualty when young people's responsibilities at home take precedence. Our secondary learners may be working themselves to keep their families afloat as well.

## TIP 4: ACCOMMODATE PARENTS AND FAMILIES AT SCHOOL EVENTS

Conferences and parent education nights must be as accessible as possible. Not all families have access to babysitters or even consider that relevant in their culture. Educators must have coloring sheets, activities, safe snacks, and roll out the red carpet for these families. We should also adjust the ways these events look to accommodate the needs of the community.

## TIP 5: BE AWARE OF ANY ACCESS ISSUES

Something important to consider, however, is never to assume that learners have access to materials from home other than the standard school supplies that your district may require. We don't know the situation in which the learners we serve live, nor do we necessarily know their financial situation. Many teachers require that learners bring in magnets, feathers, ribbons, and other items for art projects or decorations that may not be in all homes. Just remembering to be sensitive to this goes a long way.

### TIP 6: CONNECT WITH FAMILIES YOU SERVE

Educators should strive to educate themselves around the holiday traditions of all students before planning anything that may exclude anyone. When we seek out ways to engage parents and connect with them positively, it benefits everyone—especially our students.

## Conclusion

Being responsive as an educator means that we consider our learners through a holistic lens. They are more than what they academically do, and every person contributes to the culture of the community. Within this culture, we must all find a sense of belonging to truly connect and grow alongside one another. (I include the educators and the learners in this!) Winokur (2023) discusses the impact of feelings of *belonging* for all learners on both their own educational journeys and those of everyone around us.

Earlier in this chapter, we discussed collaborative learning and how this may foster connections among learners who perhaps may not have interacted without these opportunities. When we intentionally provide these positive experiences among young people, we create an environment in which there are no strangers; all learners are members of this group, and the feelings of belonging are powerful.

When diverse perspectives are celebrated throughout the classrooms and schools, we see ourselves as being an integral part of the community. Our learners see and hear their languages in music, decorations, assemblies, and literature, and they know they are accepted and valued. Along those lines, we learn about cultures that are different from ours, and we see similarities and ways that we can connect with them.

We provide pathways to engagement and leadership. We want diverse voices represented on our student council and peer leadership. We can engage our learners as ambassadors to represent our school and warmly welcome new students to our community. Leadership opportunities are accessible to all stakeholders (learners and educators) as we feel that sense of belonging and investment in our school.

As we engage all learners in dynamic and responsive experiences, we empower all of us to reflect and keep learning.

## DISCUSSION QUESTIONS

- What experiences in your life happened outside the classroom but had an impact on your education? These may represent a positive influence or a challenge.
- What are your experiences with working in groups? Share both positive experiences and frustrations.
- Discuss a book in which you felt that something about the character or events represented your own life or experiences. Describe how that affected your engagement with this book. ●

# PROFESSIONAL LEARNING AND GROWING

CHAPTER 9

## Frontloaded Vocabulary

**advocate** (noun): Someone who publicly uses their voice and position to champion a cause of a group of people.

**pedagogy:** This is the study of the methods and practices of teaching children. ●

As educators, we are lifelong learners. Not only is it our responsibility to remain current with the latest research and best practices in the field, but we must have the mindset that we always have something new to learn about the learners and the communities we serve. It is our responsibility to remain curious and open to changing our perspectives when we learn new information.

## Professional Learning Versus Professional Development

There has been talk in our field about the difference between *professional learning* and *professional development* and the experiences associated with each (Furlong & Spina, 2022). With the explosion of opportunities that came with the pandemic, the landscape of how educators access training and information has changed in so many ways.

Historically, *professional development* (PD) has been training, workshops, or presentations mandated by an educational institution for educators. Professional development often reflects current instructional initiatives or commercial programs being implemented in a school district. This is often done in the district, but there are times when educators attend workshops or conferences off site. PD sessions are often helpful and useful for implementation of required changes or updates, but some educators report that they are not directly related to areas of choice or passion for them (Furlong & Spina, 2022). That said, it is crucial that we as educators approach any opportunity for honing our craft with an open mind and a growth mindset.

*Professional learning* (PL) may have some overlap with professional development, but the feeling of many educators is that there is more agency and choice in professional learning. This may be within the contractual hours of the school day or may be something in which educators engage independently. The connotation that PL often carries connects the activities with educator agency, motivation, and feelings of self-efficacy. Professional learning may also be less formal or regulated than professional development as well.

## Professional Book Clubs

*Professional book clubs* for teachers are great ways to engage with colleagues in conversation that is structured around a book. Topics for these books may include pedagogy and teaching strategies, representations of cultures in your community, content-area knowledge, and cultural responsiveness. Book studies may take place within your school or grade level or even through online forums with colleagues in other states or countries. One of the best book studies I (Denise) participated in was with a young adult book that represented experiences that some of our students have had; when we finished the hard conversations, we all donated the books to the middle school classroom libraries!

A newer movement in the world of educator book clubs may be to include banned books as the focus. While we most certainly all have our own views on banning books, it is important for educators to be knowledgeable about these books to be able to have critical conversations about this (hopefully temporary) shift in education. Conversations about messages in these books and ways that they may provide representation for marginalized groups can be ways to view books through a different lens. The reflection in terms of educator perspectives and potential bias when considering these books may be powerful.

The key to a successful local book club is to take the school's temperature to see where educators may want to learn more. This may be through quarterly anonymous questionnaires or through specific requests through PLCs or meetings. Climate and culture surveys may also provide insight into areas in which educators do not feel confident. Having these conversations with your mentor or informal mentors may be a springboard for safe places to ask for more engagement on a particular topic or skill. Sharing positive and educational experiences through books may be a way to open honest conversations and cultivate a culture of learning and collaboration.

These book clubs may be in areas of self-improvement, specific content areas, self-help and self-care, or ways to better connect with the school community. Much like our learners engage best when they have voice and choice, so do our colleagues. A mixture of in-person discussion and a virtual discussion board (Google Classroom or Padlet?) may fit the needs of many participants while keeping the stress of keeping up at bay. Ideally, diversity within the book club in terms of roles in education and backgrounds will provide space for some wonderful learning for everyone.

## Social Media

*Social media* as a tool for professional learning is a way that educators can connect with colleagues across the miles in a more informal way. There are times in which we may feel isolated or even stagnant as educators. This may be because of the design of our school (maybe we are the only teacher at a grade level or in a content area?) or due to a variety of other reasons. When educators connect with others alongside whom they may learn, they can re-energize themselves or even bolster their feelings of belonging and self-efficacy.

If you would like to engage in social media for professional learning, here are a few tips to keep in mind:

1. Create a professional profile and keep things education related or at least posts that positively represent you as an educator.
2. Follow administrators and school pages for local districts, as well as local universities, to make connections for networking, job opportunities, or even conferences that you may wish to attend.
3. Seek out educators who may be active on your platforms of choice and are respected in the field. They may be professional learning facilitators or even authors.

4. Don't limit yourself to one platform—but do not overextend yourself. Set aside a time that works for your schedule to catch up on your various accounts.

There are Facebook groups for every special interest group in education you can imagine. Twitter/X chats are less common than they used to be, but if you find one that interests you, join in! Social media also has some great book studies that are conducted asynchronously. LinkedIn has increased in popularity with educators and may be a way to highlight your work and network with others in the same field or geographical area. Instagram and Threads are a bit quieter in terms of educators, but TikTok has a thriving educator community.

## Webinars and Virtual Conferences

*Webinars* and *virtual conferences* have been around for years, but they took on a renewed purpose during the pandemic when travel was so restricted—and I maintain that this is part of a movement that changed the face of professional learning from that moment forward. Educators saw these opportunities for self-paced, individualized professional learning in which they were in control. They did not have to wait for approval for a substitute or a purchase order from their district. This was professional learning of their choosing that provided both content and connections with fellow educators—and often participation was free or very inexpensive.

While the content creation of these webinars is not as consistent as we are post pandemic, attending a conference virtually or even viewing a past event is easily accessible to this day. By providing virtual access to these events, educators in our field are providing points of access to professional learning that may not have been an option for people whose geographic location may have prevented their participation previously. Large conferences often offer both in-person and online library access to content to engage and include an exponentially larger number of participants.

As we consider ways to grow in our craft, we understand the impact that *politics and other factors* may have on what and how we teach. It's important to note that different states have different norms and standards for professional learning. As educators, it is our duty to understand these norms that are particular to our area and become informed consumers of information in terms of the decisions. To be clear, we may not support all or parts of these initiatives and must decide to follow curricula or programs that we may agree with. This is a challenge for many educators and—for some—it is even more of a reason why connecting with others across the miles may be helpful.

When policies are debated that affect education, it is every educator's duty to become informed on the historical and future implications of potential laws or changes that may be put into place. Fortunately, we have our voices and our advocacy platforms to stand firm on issues that are necessary for our students to get the best education possible.

Over the career of an educator, one will see many shifts in the prevailing way of teaching nearly everything. We often discuss it as the pendulum swinging. When things go too far in one direction, one hopes that it "evens out" a bit eventually. Some educational environments are not supportive of new or innovative views on teaching and learning. I have always been of the mind that it is my own responsibility to learn what I truly believe is good teaching and best practice—even if I must formally follow a program that does not embrace what I think is best for my learners.

## Professional Learning Communities

A current movement in many school districts is to engage educators in *professional learning communities* (PLCs) to establish these types of professional supports and conversations as a valued part of the weekly or monthly schedule. PLCs at the local/school/district level often take place during the teachers' contractual day, and sometimes educators belong to more than one PLC at a time. Some PLCs are equivalent to grade-level teams or content-area groups, while others are determined by scheduling or interest groups. Educators also often must set professional goals at the beginning of the year, and this may drive PLCs as well.

The notion of participating in PLCs as certified educators is grounded in the idea that professional learning and growth is essential throughout one's career and should happen in a variety of formats. PLCs may be a place in which curriculum is discussed, data is analyzed, specific needs of learners are shared, or school events are planned. Sometimes administration, guidance counselors, school nurses, or other related service educators may attend to ensure a structured session that may be particular to the team's needs. *Structured PLCs* may include more formal training on topics, such as assessments, meeting diverse needs of learners, or content-specific themes.

### CREATING AND COORDINATING EFFECTIVE PLCs

If your state has a new teacher mentorship program, there may be regularly scheduled meetings for you to either meet as a PLC with other beginner teachers or with your mentor. Your mentor is ideally a seasoned educator whose teaching assignment shares some similarities to yours. According to Knight (2015), educators may serve as *formal mentors* via one of these official programs, or they may serve as *informal mentors*. Informal mentors are the other educators who support novice teachers in many ways. These may include sharing the procedures and norms of the school, providing different perspectives and suggestions for success in the classroom, and fostering feelings of support and community. Ideally, PLCs are the perfect place to connect with others who may become informal mentors for one another.

If your district or state does not endorse formal PLCs, this may be an opportunity to connect with other novice teachers or people in your grade level/content area informally. This may be a local coffee-shop meeting or something that is long distance via video call. While some may feel that this is a frivolous use of time, this may truly be a way for educators to feel connected or supported by others who are experiencing similar challenges. For those educators whose states or districts may not be supportive of this type of collaboration, this professional learning is free and may provide the lifeline that one may need at any part of one's teaching career.

## Expanded Opportunities for Professional

While it is crucial for all educators to maintain boundaries between their work and personal lives for many reasons, the occasional social/professional events are sometimes invigorating and empowering.

> *"An integral part of the teaching profession is learning. You must never stop learning about the learners who are in your care. You are not just helping them learn content. Your learners are in a critical stage of developing a mental attitude that will determine how they interpret, process, and respond to situations. In order for you to guide them, you must be in a continuous process of learning yourself. If there comes a day when you feel you know everything, that should be the day you get out."*
>
> —Donna, teacher and BOE member, Massachusetts

There are many ways that serving our community and field may also provide us with opportunities for professional learning. Serving on local education committees, working at a soup kitchen, or volunteering at the library may be great ways to learn in a way that feeds your soul. Local advocacy agencies that particularly service children and adolescents may be ways to learn about the services that are available in your county. Services for immigrants or tutoring adults may also be satisfying and educational for you as well.

If you work in a state that has a union or a different type of organization in which educators come together in support, this may be a useful way to network while bettering your community. Other educators find state or local affiliates of national organizations to support with their service; over the years, I have delighted in learning alongside my colleagues in professional learning organizations.

It is important as an educator new to the professional to understand that we cannot learn it all—all at once. There will be things that are a focus in your first years, and then your expertise will expand as your experience grows. No one expects people to be experts in everything right away. A lifelong learner will always find something new to learn, and they will find joy in that.

## Technology and Artificial Intelligence (AI)

One of the positive outcomes of teaching during the pandemic was the hands-on and authentic learning with different types of technology for both educators and learners. So many districts pivoted to virtual instruction, and professional development in technology was of top priority. Technology shifted from being an *add-on* or a choice to being a vital part of our communication with learners and their families.

> *"I find it challenging to find the right 'level' of professional development for technology in education. Sometimes they are too basic for me, and others are too advanced. But I have found that this is an area I'd like to grow in, and I keep trying."*
>
> —Gillian, EL/ML educator, New Jersey

As it is now the norm to utilize forums like Google Classroom or Schoology in many classrooms and often learners have access to Chromebooks or tablets, many educators are at the point where they feel they can expand on their knowledge in technology to engage the learners they serve in different ways.

An area where education is changing quickly is the use of artificial intelligence (AI) by educators and learners. Many feel threatened by the unknowns associated with AI, and much of the conversation regarding it has a negative view of how educators must *control* use of it. According to Poth (2023), to keep up with AI and its updates, educators must adapt and evolve to stay on top of it. What we knew about AI even two months ago is not the same AI that exists today.

As AI is receptive to feedback and constant updating, some view the assistance that educators may get almost as an electronic collaboration with others. Some educators search for ideas for lessons or different ways to engage their learners. Others may use AI assistance for writing recommendation letters, searching for literature reviews, or for checking sources. Another potential use for AI for educators may be personalized "tutoring" that one may access, such as learning other languages or suggestions for differentiation in instruction. In fact, Willmore (2023) describes ways that learners can interact with avatars that represent scientific phenomena from a distance and learn about animals and the environment in ways that they never could have otherwise.

Notably, AI is often associated with cheating, and it may provide inaccurate or biased information. Educators often may use *AI detectors* as ways to determine if learners' writings or projects are their own or generated through AI. Assessments are being updated to either engage learners in AI or attempt to prevent its use. As consumers are navigating this ever-changing world, true understanding of the implications of these policies is critical to be responsive to learners.

Above all, it is critical to know the AI policies of your district and your university. While we as educators may be learning and growing in our use of AI, we must be cautious not to engage in practices that violate rules of procedures of our institutions. The ethical use of AI is an important part of this conversation. According to The United Nations Educational, Scientific, and Cultural Organization (UNESCO, 2024), the protection of young children requires an age restriction of 13 years old to engage with it. While young learners may be knowledgeable about these technologies, educators must be cognizant of limitations in engaging them in our classrooms.

## Advocacy

As we move along our paths as educators, we take on different roles. As novice educators we are working through curricula, managing behaviors positively, and learning about the cultures, values, and perspectives in our school community (even if it is an area where we grew up!). We are making connections with our colleagues and contributing positively to our school environment. This may mean attending events after school, coaching, or advising clubs. We may not realize it during this part of our journey, but these are the first steps we take in becoming advocates for our learners and their families.

What exactly does *advocate* mean (particularly in education), and what are some possible connotations? I often view advocacy as using my voice to effect change for the benefit of others. These include the learners and families I serve, my colleagues, and the school community. To be an advocate, one must be well informed on the issues, have a true understanding of the community and culture, and hold positive connections with the stakeholders within a place of trust.

Advocates cannot be people who decide that there is a problem with someone else's life situation or challenges and are determined to make changes on their behalf. Yes, at times advocates are not part of the central group who would directly benefit from changes to policy, procedures, or norms—especially in the field of education. However, true advocates will connect with the stakeholders and community members whose lives are affected and truly listen to their perspectives. To be clear, sometimes advocates feel strongly about an issue that the affected community does not support for whatever reasons. Creating an environment in which the voices of the community are valued and where their needs are at the forefront is necessary, as is working alongside community members in whatever advocacy work is done. Advocates are allies; they are not ones who take voice and choice away from others.

Crucial to note is that there is a fine line between being an advocate for the members of your school community and being a *savior.* To be clear, we as educators often come toward our advocacy from a place of privilege. We are educated, and we (hopefully) have stable work with health insurance and other benefits. While our profession is not known for its top-tier salaries (sorry!), we generally earn regular pay checks that are consistent in our wages. We can view taking risks and raising our voices from a different point of view than some of the communities we hope to support. Our voice and privilege may give the communities we serve a platform, but it is their voice that must be at the forefront. Advocacy comes from a place of allyship rather than saviorism.

## The Mindful Educator

In the first years, educators often learn much about themselves as humans, if they take the time to reflect. That *reflection* is sometimes difficult to do when adrenaline is flowing and when they are just trying to stay afloat. They don't want to focus on what they may be doing wrong, which may be the reason they avoid intentional reflection. However, nonjudgmental notes or journal entries can be revisited later to consider updates or changes that may be made in the future.

This reflection may also cover things that we may need as humans in terms of mindful practice and self-care. Careful consideration of our bodies, feelings, and reactions is extremely useful when examined alongside our work with our learners. Are there things that trigger us? Are there ways we can handle situations differently or more effectively? Akhavan et al. (2021) maintains that targeted professional learning by teachers in mindfulness practices shows improvements in communication and interactions with students as well as teacher stress.

Self-affirmations are also an excellent way to set the tone for the day or to remind ourselves (and our students!) of our own potential and talents. According to Epton et al. (2014), research suggests that affirmations may have a positive effect on health-related feelings and behaviors. Intentional time in which affirmations are verbalized and acknowledged can be one way to be a mindful role model for both your own benefit and for your students.

Since beginning intentional mindful practice in my classroom, I started modeling skills for my learners that no one ever taught me as a child. Taking an extra moment to share breathing techniques before an assessment or even discussing one's feelings may be powerful ways to empower children as humans who listen to their own bodies. Many times, the vocabulary associated with mindful practice or emotions may be something that children do not learn unless they are explicitly taught.

I found that speaking about these things in my classrooms and with my colleagues as well helped "normalize" these discussions for everyone. *"I'm feeling a bit anxious today and my stomach is a little upset. Something that calms me down is classical music, so I plan on playing some while I eat lunch."* Understanding and verbalizing that our emotions may have physical manifestations (and that is normal!) is helpful for many people to identify connections among the reactions in their bodies.

As educators, we experience stress and emotion in so many ways daily. It is so important that we foster environments in which we (and our learners) can cope positively and provide space for ourselves to self-regulate. What started out as a solo journey through mindful practice for me became a powerful way that I nurtured a supportive classroom climate.

## Growing Pains of New Educators

Much like in any life experience, novice educators find themselves in situations where they are trying to find their own voice and mission while navigating the existing norms and longtime traditions in their school. As someone new to school culture, there may be some learning curves in how one finds this balance.

It is critical to acknowledge the importance of embracing the unique gifts of novice teachers to their school communities. While they are new in the field with possibly limited experience, there are many ways in which novice teachers bring fresh ideas and up-to-date knowledge in different areas. That said, some novice teachers encounter resistance to change or new ideas. *"That's the way we've always done it."* While we cannot expect to change everything for the better immediately when we arrive in a new school or district, we can focus on small, measurable changes that may have a big impact. As we establish ourselves, we can continue making these shifts in mindset and practice on a larger scale.

*"I remember in my second year of teaching, I moved out of my trailer classroom and into a classroom inside of the school building. A colleague had just retired, and I was excited to have a new learning space. I was tasked with going through cabinets and file folders and seeing what was inside various bins. As my colleague had over 30 years of experience, there were file folders of resources, lesson plans, paperwork hiding in various places throughout the space. There were also bins of various art supplies and paper. It was a LOT to sort through! Which pieces would I hang on to? What would I need this year? Which materials were safe to get rid of right now, in order to create space for newer materials or supplies?*

*Similarly, there are times where we need to take an inventory of what practices or mindsets we still have—or that we have inherited from our school systems—that do not serve our students or families. I've had to constantly check and recheck myself when I've found myself absorbing negative and/or problematic mindsets that can (and do) exist in the air of our school hallways, data meetings, and decision-making matrices. Especially as educators and leaders who serve historically underserved students, it is critical that we examine the mindsets that drive us."*

—Carly, author, ML specialist, Illinois

As we integrate ourselves into our school communities, we learn more about the cultures of our learners, their families, and our colleagues. This may include volunteering at school events, coaching sports, and advising activities or clubs. We can also get involved by joining committees with other staff. These may be opportunities to affect change in your school community and foster connections with staff members who may be outside your immediate circle of colleagues. Considering that there are many avenues to build your knowledge base as an educator that both are in your comfort zone and outside it is critical in your professional and personal growth.

I have often found that the most unconventional paths to learning have been the most rewarding.

Understanding the continuing education norms or requirements of your district or state is important as you navigate your first years. If you are encouraged to get additional teaching credentials or advanced degrees, please think carefully about your long-term goals and your educational passions and see where they intersect with what is required of you for maintaining your teaching license. Keep in touch with your university contacts and follow their paths for inspiration. Engage with your mentors to design your path and get the most out of these experiences as possible.

## Conclusion

The mindset of a lifelong learner is what drives educators to evolve and learn alongside their learners. Where you begin as a novice teacher may often not be where you stay; this goes for geography, perspectives, and mindset. A great practice may be to reflect on your philosophy of education (perhaps you wrote one in your teacher education program) at the end of each year. Include both short-term and long-term goals and be open to change if that is where your heart takes you. If you are committed to any specific goals, then take that time to plan how you will attain them.

## DISCUSSION QUESTIONS

- What are your favorite topics for professional learning, and why do you enjoy them?
- Where do you see yourself in five years? What types of professional learning and growing will help you reach that goal?
- How do you handle situations in which you feel professional development does not apply to you or your position? ●

# THRIVING IN THIS PROFESSION

CHAPTER **10**

As we gear up for the beginning of each school year, the whirlwind of excitement and activity in our schools is palpable. The sounds of teachers and staff preparing for their new classes are full of promise for a successful school year. In the flurry of designing bulletin boards, unpacking supplies, and ringing telephones are the first-time teachers, both smiling and a bit sick to their stomachs at the same time. You see, for them it's more than a new school year; it's a new chapter in their lives. It's time to prove that they can do it! They *can* be caring, knowledgable, and effective teachers. They *can* make a difference in the lives of their learners. They *can* make it through the first week (and the next and the next!).

Over my career, we have worked with many novice teachers, and I have learned so much from them. Their enthusiasm for learning is infectious, and they are certainly up on the latest research and techniques. But there are a few things that I wish I knew when I first became a teacher (other than to run in the opposite direction!). Trust me, you will find your rhythm and your unique style, and this will serve you and your learners well.

## Find Your Village

As the saying goes, "It takes a village to support a new teacher . . ." (or something like that!). Your village as a new teacher can provide you with the necessary support to feel successful and supported. This village may shift or change but will continue to be valuable to you throughout your career. This support may come to you from a variety of directions, or you may have to seek it out. Either way, these connections can help bolster you when you need a helping hand.

You may be starting your teaching career with many other new teachers alongside you, or you may be the lone newbie in your school. Either way, connecting with other educators who can share experiences with you is crucial. While you may be nervous to reach out for assistance or establish new professional relationships, you will find that many colleagues are happy to collaborate with new teachers. Connections through new teacher orientation, grade-level meetings, run-ins in the hallway or faculty room, and even carrying with you those friends from your teacher education programs are great places to start building your networks. These teachers may support you in person, on social media, via texts, smoke signals, however you foster those connections. Hopefully, these relationships are reciprocal in terms of sharing experiences and learning from one another.

Please know that you may still have a lot to learn but you also have much to share as well. The most effective educator support systems are those where everyone can learn from others. Seeking out people who are sincere as lifelong learners and who are willing to accept help may be the key to your successful partnerships.

With this being said, it's important to understand that having a "teacher bestie" does not make or break your year. I have had times in which I had great friendships with my colleagues, and we would spend time together with our families outside of work. There were other years where I was friendly and professional with my colleagues, but I left it in the school building. In other words, don't put a lot of pressure on yourself to create these relationships within your building or district. Some of my closest teacher friends live in other states or countries—and I laugh and learn with them as well!

> *"Never be afraid to lean on others for advice. Chances are if you are struggling with something, that the teacher down the hall has experienced the same thing. I'm in my third year of teaching now and I find that there are things that my grade-level team all try to improve together as a team."*
>
> —Matt, educator and coach, New Jersey

Other members of your village include your mentor, grade-level, or content-area colleagues, paraprofessionals, administrators, coaches, custodians, secretaries, food services workers, and crossing guards (you get the idea). *There is no one from whom you cannot learn, no matter their role in your district or community.*

## Reflect, Reflect, Reflect

As you begin in this amazing profession, record those memories and experiences in whatever way works for you. These personal reflections about teaching, learning, connecting, and growing will help you see how far you've come—and where you want to go. You may keep a journal of lessons learned and be disciplined about writing in it every day. Or maybe you will write a positive memory from each day and put it in a jar to read at the end of the school year. You will surely find those reflections to be a treasured artifact of this "moment in time." You are surely at a pivotal time in your life!

Less personal reflections, such as notes embedded in your lesson plans, are also very useful. What worked in this lesson? What would I do differently next time? You may even return to these notes much later if you find additional materials that may work in this unit. All of this is useful because you may be doing a similar lesson at a later time, or this may shape other lessons in the future.

*"One of my assignments during student teaching was to write a reflection for my lessons, and my professor encouraged me to sit and write something at the end of each day that had nothing to do with academics. I didn't look at that notebook until after my first year of teaching had ended, and I teared up at all of the incredible things I learned about being a teacher. And, to be honest, some of the most challenging days were the times that I grew the most."*

—Susanna

Reflecting with others in your village is incredibly important as well. Different ways to set up a classroom community, techniques for guided reading, and engaging labs in science class all may be born out of conversations with your village. And let's be clear: Not every suggestion or recommendation will suit your style. But keep them in your pocket in case you ever rethink your preference at another time or if you teach a different level. Sometimes even the discourse that you have will help clear things up in your mind.

Having someone outside your school to whom you can vent or share successes is helpful as well. Sometimes someone who has a different perspective can help you through rocky times or just lend a sympathetic ear. My sister (not an educator) gives me great advice and celebrates my successes as someone who has rooted for my success my entire life. My husband and kids support my *teacher time* without question, and they are proud of the differences I make in kids' lives. These reflections with my family both recharge me and help me work through things I couldn't quite figure out on my own. Trust me, the money you will spend on coffee, tea, or other beverages will be well worth the support you receive.

Perhaps the most crucial reflections may be those that question our own interactions, perspectives, and biases. Are we truly meeting each of our learners where they are, and do we honestly believe in their potential? Are we sincere in our interactions with our learners' families and the ways that we support them? Do we advocate for all learners? Do we have a deep understanding of the cultures of our school community and how our learners carry those cultures with them in everything they do? As we journal about our experiences, these are things that can guide us as we seek to improve ourselves as educators. We—educators who reflect in these ways—are all a work in progress.

## Connections Before Curricula

Let's face it: Not every learner will enter your class just bursting with intrinsic motivation to learn every lesson you plan, as beautiful as your lessons are. Most learners may not fully comprehend the importance of what they will learn with you and the positive effect of it on the rest of their lives. Learners are not sponges, just waiting to soak up all academic things. It is through connections and relationships that learners find the motivation to put in the effort needed to progress and learn.

If it weren't for the need for connections, children could learn from robots (or artificial intelligence!). Teachers learn about the interests, strengths, challenges, and uniqueness of their learners and use those to engage them in reaching their potential. Those connections are essential to creating the classroom climate in which learners strive for success—and truly feel that they can achieve it.

*Learners who feel you care about them will want to please you and believe you have their best interests at heart.* They will trust that what you teach them is worthwhile and will be motivated to learn. I'm not trying to say that every learner every day will earn top grades or complete every assignment, but these connections are part of the recipe for engagement. If a learner does not engage one day, you will certainly try to connect him with his potential the following day.

Genuinely representing and celebrating diverse backgrounds (languages, families, abilities, identities) is a culturally responsive way to connect with your learners. Providing them with a safe space to be authentic is so important for everyone, both as individuals and as a classroom support network. This manifests in classroom connections in several ways.

Since I started to really be intentional about the books in the classroom, the languages of my learners, and the scaffolds/supports I give for all learners as they need them, I saw a shift in the classroom dynamic. Kids started asking questions about ways to say things in other languages. They would rush in when they heard news from a country that one of their classmates was from and start discussions. They would support their peers as they stepped out of their comfort zones in speaking new languages. As it became the norm to be curious and supportive of everyone, all learners seemed to be willing to take more chances themselves.

## It's OK to Make Mistakes— As Long as You Own Them

Have you ever experienced a class *catching* the teacher in a mistake? This can either be a mortifying experience for the teacher—or a positive teachable moment for all involved. One of the lessons that I learned later in my career is that mistakes are nothing of which to be ashamed. Modeling respect in terms of correcting mistakes and owning your own is such an important skill to share with your learners. The key is to embed this in your classroom culture.

This should be established on the first day of class. Teachers should elaborate on how they make mistakes, how learners make them, and that they are part of learning. No one should be permitted to correct another learner except the teacher—and only then in a supportive way. Laughing or shouting out corrections is not to be tolerated. If the teacher makes a mistake, a learner certainly can respectfully share that with him or her in the spirit of learning. Hopefully, the teacher and class can have a good laugh about the mistake and move on. If the focus on mistakes (our own and others') is to support learning, there is no joy in pointing out the errors of others. The tone of the class is "I've got you!" rather than "Gotcha!"

Should teachers focus on correcting all errors? This is a personal choice and influences your classroom climate. When learners are reading aloud or speaking, teachers might choose to correct the mistakes essential to the objective of the lesson or the story. Other mistakes—if the content is still understandable—are fine to let go. You don't want your learners to feel that every word they say is going to be corrected; no one will want to take a chance and participate. When grading written pieces, teachers should choose three pieces of constructive, actionable feedback upon which to focus on rather than giving back a paper that is torn apart with corrections. Learners may focus more on learning from their mistakes if they aren't presented with too many to consider. Again, if learners know that they can take risks and still be supported, they will be more likely to try to go out of their comfort zone.

Some educators might think, "If I let their mistakes go, how will learners learn?" This is certainly valid and depends on your teaching style, content area, and learners in your class. Correcting mistakes is sometimes connected to having high expectations for learners and the desire to ensure they learn as much as possible. Instead, reflect on what approach (or combination of approaches) would most benefit your learners and follow that path—*what is good for kids* is always the right way to do things.

## Cultivate Positive Coteacher Relationships

You may experience a variety of types of coteacher situations over your career, and you may begin your first year with this. Coteaching is when two (or more) teachers combine their respective talents in one or more classrooms for the benefit of their learners. The teachers may include the classroom general education teacher, content-area specialists, teachers of multilingual learners, teachers of learners with IEPs, reading or math specialists, basic skills teachers, related arts teachers, paraprofessionals—or more!

Much like spouses (haha!), coteachers must work hard at maintaining positive relationships through respectful communication. This honest communication must cover everything teachers do with respect to their mutual learners. Work ethics, teaching styles, and educational priorities may all be subject to negotiation among these professionals, but continual respectful discourse and compromise are key to working through these together. Teachers may have unique relationships with different coteachers, as it is critical to find the way that each can contribute their own talents to the education of their learners.

The balance of *power* in the classroom must leave room for all professionals to do their part in providing the best education possible for all learners. There is no room for teachers to be territorial, whether in terms of time with learners, grades, or the classroom's physical environment. There are many effective models of coteaching that may be followed, and these models may change on any given day or class. For a refresher on the different ways that coteaching may successfully meet diverse needs, please return to Chapter 6.

Not only does a positive coteaching relationship make for a smoother, more interactive day for teachers, but the ways that you interact with other professionals in front of learners serve as a model for the children. They witness the respectful discourse, the contributions of different people toward a common goal, and the connections that are made among the professionals and the learners. Sometimes coteachers become sincere friends, and other times coteaching is the extent of their relationships. Either is acceptable—as long as each works toward the goal of providing the best of themselves for the benefit of all learners.

## Discipline With Dignity

There is much talk about classroom management in preservice teaching programs as you read about in Chapter 4. In fact, you may have had an entire course or section of a course dedicated to managing behaviors in your classroom. While I'm not suggesting that new teachers go into their first classes without a solid plan for maintaining order in the class (perhaps not as severe as these!), establishing relationships while doing so will make them much more successful.

Classroom management that is respectful and maintains the dignity of learners is most effective. Period. No longer do we put a child's name on the board or have public displays of behavior charts because behavior struggles should not be subject to public shaming. Learners must be able to trust that if they make mistakes or have errors in judgment, they will be corrected in an appropriate way that reinforces expectations and ensures that they learn from experience.

Establishing norms and maintaining structure provides learners with the comfort of knowing what to expect, both when the class is going smoothly and when things go awry. Consistency in expectations and consequences is a critical way that teachers show kindness to their learners. They care enough about them to support them in making good decisions and challenging themselves in a positive way in the classroom.

With the importance of connections in the classroom in mind, fostering those relationships will do wonders for maintaining order and positive behaviors. Learners are more respectful of teachers who show that they care about them as individuals—and that work starts on Day 1.

## Where You Start May Not Be Where You Stay

As you start your first year as a teacher, you may feel that you arrived in your classroom through destiny, and this is where you will spend your career. Alternatively, you may have taken a position that you view as a steppingstone to another job in a different district. You may also find that your certifications allow you to transfer positions within your district and experience different aspects of educating learners.

There may be a time in your career when you decide to make a change, and there is nothing wrong with that. This may be with career advancement in mind or SEMH (social-emotional mental health) or family issues at the heart of the change. Being open to change is sometimes difficult and scary, but many times change gives us the experiences that form us as educators. I sincerely feel that your journey as an educator may have more twists and turns than you thought it would, but it is the journey you are meant to take.

*"Educators surely choose their content areas based on their strengths, but other factors may determine their 'destiny.' Did we choose our district because of the population, proximity to home, salary, safety, availability of a position, or all the above? Did we seek out districts that align with our values or teaching philosophies? Do these decisions shape us into the educator we are supposed to be—for the students we are 'supposed' to have? Or . . . do we adjust ourselves to meet the needs of the students we have?"*

—Denise

## Ration Your Passion

Your first years as a teacher will undoubtedly be the years that you spend the most time preparing lessons, feedback, and materials for your classes. That said, teacher burnout in the early years is a real problem. Finding a balance that will allow you to learn and grow as a teacher while also not living and breathing your job is essential to a long, successful career.

Sometimes our colleagues or administrators are supportive of this work-life balance, and others may experience resistance from others in terms of drawing this line in the sand. As we discussed in the preceding section, you may be in a situation in which you must make decisions with your health and your future as a teacher in mind.

By *rationing your passion*, you work hard on your craft, but you set aside time for your family and free time to maintain your SEMH in a positive way. Setting limits and boundaries is important to avoiding burnout. Keeping yourself healthy is important to yourself, your profession, and your life outside of work.

## The First Contact You Make With Parents Should Be Positive

Effective educators recognize that an important member of a learner's support team is their parents. This home-school connection is key to help learners understand the importance of their learning, especially if parents follow up with their children at home about their progress.

However, sometimes teachers do not choose to actively engage parents outside of obligatory conferences until there is a problem. To establish positive relationships between teachers and parents, though, it is better to contact them before there is an issue. We want to create that feeling of teamwork in a positive fashion so that parents see that we are all on the same team: their child's team. Later, if you need to reach out to parents for behavioral or academic support for their child, they recognize that you are not *picking on* their child and that you sincerely want to help them succeed. Those bonds of trust between families, learners, and educators set learners up for success.

These communications may be in the form of phone calls, emails, cards to their house, texts on approved apps, or other means. These interactions do not have to take much time (quick written messages may be faster than phone calls!), but they may have lasting consequences for the familial support you see.

## Keep Calm and Carry On

Problems with tech? Classroom management challenges? Lesson flop? It's gonna happen! It's easy to get frustrated or nervous when these things happen, but it's important to keep your cool and work on getting your class back on track if possible. Other times, changing course in the middle of a lesson is a reasonable way to deal with these issues. The key is showing your learners that grace under pressure is a positive way to deal with adversity, and the ways that you model this behavior will certainly be an example for them.

Our learners must view us as human beings who make mistakes and who have feelings, in addition to being educators. With that being said, you must be sure that you maintain your position as facilitator without the learners feeling as if they are in a position of power if things out of your control happen. There are some learners who, when they see the teacher is struggling, may attempt to divert your attention or make the situation worse. Maintain your composure (being honest about what's falling apart!), and then model positive behavior about how you are keeping control and moving in a positive direction.

## Give a "Hand Up" Whenever You Have the Opportunity

As you are finding your confidence and learning your craft as a teacher, you may find that you are in a situation in which you can help a colleague who may be struggling. This may be in the form of participating in that teacher's *village* by letting them vent, helping with lesson plans, sharing space or materials, or just bringing them the occasional cup of coffee.

Keeping the perspective in which we lead with kindness and compassion in our role as an educator will color everything we do with everyone with whom we interact. This *hand up* may also be for a learner, a learner's parent, a staff member, or even an administrator. A *hand up* would be when you give assistance to someone else (even if you are in the same boat). By establishing yourself as a positive, helpful, and dependable member of your school community, you are fostering a culture in which admitting one needs help is met with support rather than judgment. That is powerful.

Lifting fellow educators not only helps them, but the learners benefit from having a supported teacher. Often the conversations we have with others are beneficial to ourselves as well. There are sometimes long-lasting ripples of positivity when we are generous of ourselves.

## Don't Stop Thinking About the Future

In the beginning of our careers, we often are only concerned with the next days, weeks, months. However, when we consider our commitment to a career as an educator, we think of how we evolve and spend much of our working years in this profession. While that may not seem imminent at this time, the small (and big!) things we do now are part of our mindset as someone who is an educator for the long haul.

One of the ways we invest in our future may be furthering our education or attaining different credentials. This may positively affect our salaries or give us opportunities to grow within our roles. As you reflect during these first years of teaching, you may revisit the *educational philosophy* that you no doubt wrote in college. Your goals and interests may change or they may become stronger. Take this time to discover what sparks your interests and passions in education—and follow those paths.

As a teacher at the beginning (read: bottom) of the pay scale, it's difficult for many to be disciplined enough to begin planning for retirement. However, if you don't begin that retirement investment right away, there will always be other reasons to put it off—until you're ready to retire! Your colleagues can guide you in beginning your 403b or whichever type of system you will use. Begin right away and contribute as much as you can out of each paycheck. Your older self will be so grateful!

## Keep Current

It's important to keep learning, even if you may have finished your teacher preparation program. While some educators thrive on reading the latest academic journal articles or pursuing additional degrees or certifications, others may not find that this is the ideal way for them to stay knowledgable of best practices in the field. However, there are many ways that educators report continuing their own learning journeys in ways that are more accessible.

Informal book clubs are excellent ways to connect with other educators and learn more casually. There are many professional trade books that lend themselves to great discussions among colleagues—both locally and via Zoom or social media. Another great option for book clubs is to read children's or young adult literature that may be mirrors for your learners. These are engaging ways to better learn about the cultures and communities in your district.

Educators have come to love podcasts and webinars that feature experts in the field. They are accessible and often conversational in tone, so they are perfect for listening in the car or while you are walking or exercising. I have even come to feel that these are part of my own *self-care* as I indulge in listening to them.

As years go on and you become more adept at managing your professional time, you can join professional organizations that can help you network and learn alongside educators in similar situations. These organizations may be local ones that are grassroots in nature, or they may be at the state or national level. These professional connections can help energize you in your own learning and growing. We covered professional learning in more detail in Chapter 9.

## Go Out of Your Way to Always Show All Staff Appreciation and Respect

There's a saying regarding feelings about how we treat others: *"It's important to treat the custodian as well as you would treat the CEO."* It's important to remember that everyone wants to come to work and feel that they and their work are valued. It is often tempting to see a secretary or custodian in the hallway and speak to them immediately about whatever it is that you need from them—without greeting them as human bcings or friends first. Your colleagues are more important than simply what they can do for you. Period.

Each person who works in a school has a *specific* and *important* role that benefits the learners. With this in mind, no one is less important than another, and everyone should be afforded the same respect as one would hope to enjoy themselves.

## Be kind to Yourself

> *"You will not love your job every day, and that is perfectly ok. Don't ever feel guilty for those days you feel defeated, when a parent was angry with you, when you felt overwhelmed, or when your lesson plan didn't land perfectly. We've all been there. But if you have more great days than crummy days, you're in good shape."*
>
> —Jody, former EL/ML teacher, Florida

Though it is easier said than done, it is important to not be so hard on yourself in this profession. We want to be the best we possibly can be, and we often think that this *best* is something that we may never attain. We think if our learners misbehave or say they don't like us that we are terrible teachers or it's something that we did wrong. We also take chronic absences and test failures personally. Here are a few things to keep in mind when those thoughts occur:

- You are the best teacher *you* can be right now at this moment. Make no excuses for the educator you are today. More growth will happen as time passes, and with that time and growth, you will become even better.

- Learners might view the most lenient teachers who put the fewest demands on them as being the nicest or the *best* teachers now, but it's the teachers who challenged them and with whom they learned the most who will be appreciated later.
- Graciously accept help and support. Sometimes it's difficult to accept that we do need assistance. One day you will be the colleague who is generous with your time and talents. Teachers pay it forward better than any people in any other profession.
- You are the exact teacher that your learners need at this particular time. You are more than good enough. You care about your learners and their success. You make a positive impact. Imposter syndrome is real—do not let it take over!

## Conclusion

> *"Love your kids, even the tough ones. Try to find that glimmer of goodness in all of them. Once you find it, encourage them to let it shine. Some of your most challenging students will tell you, sometimes years later, that you were their favorite teacher, because they always knew deep down that you cared."*
>
> —Jody, former EL/ML teacher, Florida

The days are long, but the years are short. You are embarking on the most incredible career there is with such potential for changing the world. At this point, you may be taking your job day by day—but those days add up to a career, and that career is special and meaningful to many lives.

As we are struggling through those difficult Wednesdays, just hoping to make it to the weekend, the days and weeks seem to drag. TGIF!! However, reflecting on the school year, it is inevitable that the teachers look back on how quickly it flew. Remembering to be in the moment with your learners and not to wish the year away waiting for the weekend, the next day off, or the dismissal bell is key to enjoying your job. You can change lives; relish that role and embrace your calling!

## DISCUSSION QUESTIONS

- What is your purpose in the field of education? What are your goals?
- How will you know you are *successful* in this field? What are the measures of success in your experience? ●

# REFERENCES


Akhavan, N., Goree, J. M., & Walsh, N. (2021). The benefit of mindfulness professional development for elementary teachers: Considerations for district and school level leaders. *Open Journals in Education, 6*(1), 24–42.

Brown, C. (2021, February 23). *Equity and assessment.* Center for the Professional Education of Teachers. https://cpet.tc.columbia.edu/news-press/equity-and-assessment

Cherry, K. (2023, February 22). *Lev Vygotsky's life and theories.* VeryWell Mind. https://www.verywellmind.com/lev-vygotsky-biography-2795533

Csikszentmihalyi, M. (1990). *Flow: The psychology of optimal experience.* Harper & Row.

Csikszentmihalyi, M., & Betts, K. (2023, November 14). *Flow, motivation & learning.* interact123. https://www.interact123.com/post/flow-motivation-learning

Davenport, K. (2018, November 14). *The benefits of offering students choice in assessment.* Medium. https://medium.com/its-literacy/the-benefits-of-offering-students-choice-in-assessment-b7458fa54b8c

Diamond, J. B., Randolph, A., & Spillane, J. P. (2004). Teachers' expectations and sense of responsibility for student learning: The importance of race, class, and organizational habitus. *Anthropology & Education Quarterly, 35*(1), 75–98.

Dorroh, J. (2019). *How to bring student choice to assessment in science classes.* Edutopia. https://www.edutopia.org/article/bringing-student-choice-assessment-science-classes

Elliot, J. (2016). *A collar in my pocket: Blue eyes/Brown eyes exercise.* CreateSpace Independent Publishing Platform.

Epton, T., Harris, P. R., Kane, R., von Koningsbruggen, G. M., & Sheeran, P. (2014). The impact of self-affirmation on health-behavior change: A meta-analysis. *Health Psychology, 34*(3), 187–196. https://pubmed.ncbi.nlm.nih.gov/25133846/

Fergus, E. (2022). Confronting our beliefs about poverty and discipline. *Phi Delta Kappan, 100*(5), 31–34.

Furlong, D. (2022a). A place for everyone: Inclusion for multilingual learners. *NJTESOL/NJBE Annual Voices Journal.* https://voices.njtesol-njbe.org/annual-voices-journal-2022/a-place-for-everyone/

Furlong, D. (2022b). *Voices of newcomers: Experiences of multilingual learners.* EduMatch Publishing.

Furlong, D., & Spina, C. (2022). Holistic professional learning in times of crisis. In A. Wilmot & C. Thompson (Eds.), *Handbook of research on activating middle executives' agency to lead and manage during times of crisis* (pp. 274–302). IGI Global.

Ginwright, S. (2018, May 31). *The future of healing: Shifting from trauma informed care to healing centered engagement.* Medium. https://ginwright.medium.com/the-future-of-healing-shifting-from-trauma-informed-care-to-healing-centered-engagement-634f557ce69c

Ginwright, S. (2021, February 19). *From trauma-informed to healing-centered engagement: A youth-work teach-in with Dr. Shawn Ginwright.* https://www.youtube.com/watch?v=NxTSIlWUeg8&t=1437s

Gorski, P. (2011). Unlearning deficit ideology and the scornful gaze: Thoughts on authenticating the class discourse in education. *Counterpoints, 402,* 152–173. http://www.jstor.org/stable/42981081

Hallahan, D. P., Pullen, P. C., Kauffman, J. M., & Badar, J. (2020, February 28). Exceptional learners. In *Oxford research encyclopedia of education.*

Hammond, Z. (2016). *Culturally responsive teaching and the brain: Promoting authentic engagement and rigor among culturally and linguistically diverse students.* Corwin.

Hernández, L. E., & Darling-Hammond, L. (2022). *Creating identity-safe schools and classrooms.* Learning Policy Institute. https://doi.org/10.54300/165.102

Howe, W. A., & Lisi, P. L. (2023). *Becoming a multicultural educator: Developing awareness, gaining skills, taking action.* Sage.

Hoy, A. W., & Spero, R. B. (2005). Changes in teacher efficacy during the early years of teaching: A comparison of four measures. *Teaching and teacher education, 21*(4), 343–356.

Huynh, T., & Skelton, B. (2023). *Long-term success for experienced multilinguals.* Corwin.

Kampen, M. (2022, May 31). *6 co-teaching models that can positively impact your classroom.* Prodigy. https://www.prodigygame.com/main-en/blog/co-teaching-models/

Knight, J. (2015). *Better conversations: Coaching ourselves and each other to be more credible, caring, and connected.* Corwin.

Ladson-Billings, G., & Brown, K. (2007). Curriculum and cultural diversity. *The Sage handbook of curriculum and instruction* (p. 153).

Lehman, C., Orange-Jones, K. C., & Lacy-Schoenberger, E. (2021). Lose the language of "learning loss." *Voices From the Middle, 28*(4), 26–29.

Long, C. (2016, January 26). *The far-reaching effects of implicit bias in the classroom | NEA.* National Education Association. https://www.nea.org/nea-today/all-news-articles/far-reaching-effects-implicit-bias-classroom

Orange, K. C. (2018). *Good teaching is good teaching: Teachers understanding of evaluation and teacher self-efficacy* [Doctoral dissertation, Rutgers University-Graduate School of Education].

Poth, R. D. (2023, November 9). Effective professional development on AI. *Edutopia.* https://www.edutopia.org/article/ai-professional-development-helps-teachers-tech-integration

Ruhl, C. (2023, August). What is intelligence in psychology? *Simply Psychology.*

https://www.simplypsychology.org/intelligence.html

Schaeffer, K. (2021, December 10). *America's public school teachers are far less racially and ethnically diverse than their students*. Pew Research Center. https://www.pewresearch.org/short-reads/2021/12/10/americas-public-school-teachers-are-far-less-racially-and-ethnically-diverse-than-their-students/

Shaeffer, S. (2019). Inclusive education: A prerequisite for equity and social justice. *Asia Pacific Education Review, 20*, 186–192.

Snyder, S., & Fenner, D. S. (2021). *Culturally responsive teaching for multilingual learners: Tools for equity*. Corwin.

Spencer, J. (2016, February 23). *How to move beyond a deficit mindset*. John Spencer. https://spencerauthor.com/how-to-move-beyond-deficit-mindse/

Spencer, J. (2017, December 9). *Five ways to boost student engagement with flow theory*. Medium. https://medium.com/@spencerideas/five-ways-to-boost-student-engagement-with-flow-theory-ea68064be708

Staake, J. (2023, March 2). *Types of assessments for education (and how to use them)*. We Are Teachers. https://www.weareteachers.com/types-of-assessments/

Stronge, J. H. (2006). Teacher evaluation and school improvement: Improving the educational landscape. *Evaluating Teaching: A Guide to Current Thinking and Best Practice, 2*, 1–23

The United Nations Educational, Scientific, and Cultural Organization. (2024, May 29). *Use of AI in education: Deciding the future we want*. UNESCO.org. https://www.unesco.org/en/articles/use-ai-education-deciding-future-we-want

Wiliam, D. (2011). What is assessment for learning? *Studies in Educational Evaluation, 37*(1), 3–14.

Williams, V. C. (2023). *Discipline discussions: The power of asking why*. https://sites.ed.gov/idea/behavior-as-a-form-of-communication/

Willmore, J. (2023, December 4). *AI education and AI in education*. U.S. National Science Foundation. https://new.nsf.gov/science-matters/ai-education-ai-education

Winokur, I. (2023). *Finding your pathway to belonging in education*. EduMatch Publishing.

Wisner, W. (2024, August 18). *Adverse childhood experiences: The effects of early trauma can linger well into adulthood*. Very Well Mind. https://www.verywellmind.com/what-are-aces-adverse-childhood-experiences-5219030

# INDEX

Zeitfracht Medien GmbH
Ferdinand-Jühlke-Straße 7
99095 Erfurt, Deutschland
produktsicherheit@kolibri360.de